GUNS AND CRIME

GUNS AND CRIME

Other Books in the At Issue Series:

GUNS AND CRIME

Tamara L. Roleff, *Book Editor*

David L. Bender, *Publisher*
Bruno Leone, *Executive Editor*
Bonnie Szumski, *Editorial Director*
David M. Haugen, *Managing Editor*

An Opposing Viewpoints® Series

Greenhaven Press, Inc.
San Diego, California

Library of Congress Cataloging-in-Publication Data

Guns and crime / Tamara L. Roleff, book editor.
        p.   cm. — (At issue)
    Includes bibliographical references and index.
    ISBN 0-7377-0153-6 (lib. : alk. paper). —
    ISBN 0-7377-0152-8 (pbk. : alk. paper)
    1. Firearms and crime—United States. 2. Gun control—United States. I. Roleff, Tamara L., 1959– . II. Series: At issue (San Diego, Calif.)
    HV7436.G8773   2000
    363.3'3'0973—dc21   99-37174
                                                                  CIP

©2000 by Greenhaven Press, Inc., PO Box 289009,
San Diego, CA 92198-9009

Printed in the U.S.A.

Table of Contents

Introduction

On April 20, 1999, any illusion that schools were a sanctuary from harm was permanently shattered at Columbine High School in Littleton, Colorado. Two boys, Eric Harris, 18, and Dylan Klebold, 17, arrived at school wearing their usual black trench coats. Underneath their trench coats, however, was an arsenal of weapons—two sawed-off 12-gauge shotguns, a 9-mm semiautomatic rifle, and a TEC-DC 9-mm semiautomatic handgun. Students cowered under desks and tables and behind locked classroom doors as Klebold and Harris stalked athletes, minorities, and others to kill. Police later estimated the boys fired 900 rounds of ammunition during their one-hour shooting spree. When the SWAT team finally declared the school under control five hours later, they found twelve students and one teacher dead, as well as Klebold and Harris, who had turned their weapons on themselves.

The tragedy at Columbine High School seemed to reduce the nation's tolerance for guns. Polls conducted after the Columbine massacre found 67 percent to 80 percent of Americans believed that the availability of guns should be restricted. Gun shows were a particular target for new restrictions, as all four firearms used by Klebold and Harris had been purchased at these shows. A loophole in the Brady Bill—which requires criminal background checks for all gun purchases—exempts gun shows, pawn shops, and sales between individuals from background checks.

Soon after the Colorado school shooting, the U.S. Senate made an effort to close the loophole. In May 1999, Vice President Al Gore cast the tie-breaking vote to pass a Senate bill to require mandatory criminal background checks on all sales at gun shows and when guns are redeemed at pawn shops. However, the measure stalled in the House of Representatives, and two months after the high school shooting, Democrats killed the measure rather than pass a bill that weakened current gun-control provisions.

Supporters of gun control maintain that requiring criminal background checks for gun sales at gun shows would save lives. According to Sarah Brady, chairwoman of Handgun Control Inc., background checks at gun shows are "common-sense controls on gun purchases" that would dry up "the illegal market for guns that supplies weapons to minors and criminals." Gun shows are an "arms bazaar," she adds, that

> provide a haven for criminals and illegal gun dealers who want to skirt federal gun laws and buy and sell guns on a cash-and-carry, no-questions-asked basis.

Brady points out that criminals who bought firearms at gun shows without undergoing background checks include Klebold and Harris; Timothy McVeigh, who bombed the federal building in Oklahoma City in 1995; David Koresh, the Branch Davidian religious leader who, along with his followers, was involved in a siege and shoot-out with the FBI in 1993; and Gian Luigi Ferri, who shot and killed eight people at a San Francisco law firm in 1993.

Gun-control advocates also cite a 1999 report by the Bureau of Alcohol, Tobacco, and Firearms (ATF) and the Department of Justice that found that gun shows are a major source of weapons for felons, who are prohibited by law from owning or possessing guns. According to the report, nearly half of the ATF's investigations at gun shows involved felons who bought or sold guns. In one-third of these cases, the guns were later used in a crime. But what gun-control advocates find truly astounding is that more than 54,000 firearms were bought and sold in the 314 incidents scrutinized by the report.

Opponents of gun control argue that passing new laws such as the one requiring background checks at gun shows would do little to stop gun violence. Some opponents contend that requiring background checks at gun shows would not have prevented Klebold and Harris, McVeigh, Koresh, Ferri, or others from purchasing their weapons, as they had no criminal record when they purchased their firearms. John Lott, author of *More Guns, Less Crime: Understanding Crime and Gun-Control Laws*, points out that gun dealers who sell at gun shows are required to conduct the same background checks as they do in their stores; only individuals who sell guns from their private collections are permitted to sell weapons without the required background checks and would have been affected by the new law, he asserts. According to Lott, all the owners and buyers would need to do to avoid the background check is to make the transaction outside the gun show. In order to regulate private sales, the federal government would have to register all guns, Lott explains, an option that would be unacceptable to millions of gun owners.

Instead of passing a new law to regulate gun shows, Lott and other gun-control opponents argue that existing laws should be enforced. Lott asserts that Harris and Klebold, in their shooting rampage at the high school,

> violated at least seventeen state and federal weapons-control laws. Nationwide, there are more than 20,000 gun-control laws that regulate everything from who can own a gun and how it can be purchased to where one can possess or use it.

More gun-control laws, he contends, would not have prevented the shooting at Columbine High School or other similar crimes.

Gun-control advocates and opponents do agree that crime is a serious problem in the United States. What they disagree on is whether the prevalence of guns in American society contributes to crime by making guns easily available to criminals, or prevents violent crime by allowing law-abiding citizens to protect themselves from criminals. *At Issue: Guns and Crime* examines the effectiveness of gun-control laws designed to decrease violent crime as well as other gun issues.

1

Fewer Guns Would Make Society Safer

Richard Cohen

Richard Cohen is a syndicated columnist for the Washington Post.

The Constitution in no way whatsoever guarantees minors the right to bear arms. Allowing children to have access to guns easily results in tragedies such as mass shootings at schools. By removing guns from society, and therefore from the hands of criminals and children, the risk of violent crime will be greatly reduced and society will be safer.

On the radio, I heard a disc jockey wonder if the Colorado school tragedy [in which two teenage boys shot and killed twelve students, a teacher, and then themselves in April 1999] was somehow the result of day care—parents working too much. I heard another person say something about the Gothic cult and the Internet and how maybe they were responsible for what happened. Pick your theory. The fact remains that we may never know what caused two kids to go so berserk. We do know, though, that no matter what influenced them, they had guns. This is how they did the killing.

Guns and kids

The conclusion is so obvious—and, I concede, so hackneyed by now—that I hesitate to state it. Given a change in location and the number of fatalities, it is more or less what I wrote after the last school slaughter, the one at Thurston High School in Springfield, Oregon, [in May 1998]. Yet it bears repeating: The constitutional right to bear arms cannot—and was never intended—to apply to screwed-up high school kids with a Wagnerian bent. They in no way comprise that phrase in the Constitution, "a well-regulated militia."

The National Rifle Association and like-minded groups will say that the Littleton, Colorado, tragedy is an anomaly—the sort of thing that happens rarely, although when it does it attracts lots of attention. They have a point. They will say also that the occasional abuse of a right is no

Reprinted from Richard Cohen, "The Guns Must Go," *The Washington Post National Weekly Edition*, April 26, 1999, with permission. Copyright ©1999, The Washington Post Writers Group.

cause to repeal that right for the rest of us. In this, as well, they will seem to have a point. They do not.

Consider some of the early stories coming out of Littleton: The school had no metal detectors, no uniformed cops roaming the hallways. In some accounts, the lack of security was reported in a can-you-believe-it? tone of voice. But in a different era, that tone of voice itself would have been inexplicable. Time was in America when no high school, no public building whatever, had metal detectors. We could amble into any building we wanted with anything we wanted. We were not always so afraid of guns.

But we are now. The Littleton episode is just the most recent school massacre. Recall the ones at Springfield, Jonesboro, Edinboro and Fayetteville, Pomona, Paducah, Pearl and Bethel. These are bucolic names seemingly lifted out of some 1940s song about railroads and their quaint stops. But they are places where guns got into the hands of crazy kids and tragedy resulted. That is always the bottom line: guns and kids. It is a dangerous, combustible mixture.

The fewer the guns, the fewer the violent crimes and, almost certainly, the fewer the murders.

New York City and much of the nation are now mulling over the death of Amadou Diallo, a West African immigrant shot 19 times by the police [in February 1999]. It was a mistake. He was unarmed, but the cops purportedly thought he had a gun. The tragedy has produced a national debate about the role of the police, and specifically in New York the city's vaunted Street Crime Unit. Its job—its main task—is simple: Get the guns off the street.

To an amazing degree, New York has done so. In 1992 the city had 2,200 murders. In 1998 it had 600. Undoubtedly, many factors account for those happy numbers, but certainly one is the work of the Street Crime Unit. Alone it accounted for 40 percent of the guns seized by the police in New York.

Take a gun and you abort a crime. Stop a suspect, find a gun, and you have deterred crime, maybe a murder. The fewer the guns, the fewer the violent crimes and, almost certainly, the fewer the murders. Get the guns off the streets and the streets are safer. Guns don't protect us; guns threaten us. No one holds up a bank with a knife. Who ever heard of a drive-by knifing? We are a society awash with guns—222 million of them, we are told—and they are forever falling into the wrong hands.

What is a Goth? What goes on in the heads of teenagers? The cult, the reverence for Hitler, the weird garb and the dark fascination with death are so alien that to most of us it seems we are being told of a far-away place, an alien culture where weird people do weird things. But at bottom, we are talking about teenagers, of years we all knew, of mini-cultures that are a bit crazy, where emotional extremes are common, where losers think they can turn into winners by killing themselves. To the young, suicide has a romantic aura.

To be young is, often, to be a bit crazy. For us to allow young people to be armed to boot makes us all a bit crazy, too.

2

Guns in the Right Hands Make Society Safer

David Kopel

David Kopel is the research director for the Independence Institute, a think tank that supports gun ownership as a civil liberty. He is the author of several books on gun control, including The Samurai, the Mountie, and the Cowboy: Should America Adopt the Gun Controls of Other Democracies?, *and* No More Wacos: What's Wrong with Federal Law Enforcement and How to Fix It. *Kopel is also the editor of* Guns: Who Should Have Them?

Guns in the right hands make all people safer, including those who do not own guns. Burglars in the United States are more likely to avoid occupied homes for fear of being shot by the occupants. Countries such as Canada that severely restrict gun ownership experience a significantly higher rate of "hot" burglaries—burglaries of homes and businesses that are occupied—because the criminals have little fear of getting shot by their victims. In a like manner, street crimes are reduced when law-abiding citizens are permitted to carry concealed weapons because criminals do not know who is armed and who is not.

Guns in the right hands make all good people safer—including people who don't own guns. The higher the number of responsible people who have guns ready to be used for self-defense, the safer the public is. The tremendous degree to which widespread gun ownership makes American homes safer from home invaders is one of the great unreported stories of the American gun-control debate.

Burglars fear getting shot

The United States suffers from a very high rate of violent crime, compared to most other industrial democracies. Despite recent improvement, the American crime rate is high for crimes that often involve guns (such as

Reprinted from David Kopel, "Burglary and the Armed Homestead," *Chronicles*, January 1998, with permission.

murder), and for crimes that rarely involve guns (such as rape, in which only seven percent of criminals use guns).

Yet, happily, American homes are comparatively safe from burglary. They are especially safe from "home invasion" or "hot" burglaries—that is, burglaries in which the victim is present during the burglary. As an introductory criminology textbook explains, "Burglars do not want contact with occupants; they depend on stealth for success." The textbook is correct; only 13 percent of residential burglaries in the United States are attempted against occupied homes. But this happy fact of life, so taken for granted in the United States, is not universal.

In Canada, for example, a Toronto study found that 48 percent of burglaries were against occupied homes, and 21 percent involved a confrontation with the victim. In Edmonton, about half of all burglaries are "hot." A 1982 British survey found 59 percent of attempted burglaries involved an occupied home.

Why should American criminals, who have proven that they engage in murder, rape, and robbery at a higher rate than their counterparts in other nations, display such a curious reluctance to perpetrate burglaries against occupied residences? Could part of the answer be that they are afraid of getting shot?

Guns in the right hands make all good people safer—including people who don't own guns.

In a survey of felony convicts in state prisons, 73 percent of the convicts who had committed a burglary or violent crime agreed "one reason burglars avoid houses when people are at home is that they fear being shot." Another study found that over 90 percent of burglars said that they would not even attempt a burglary in a house that they thought might be occupied.

Most scholarly studies rely on burglars who are currently incarcerated. One important study broke this mold: *Burglars on the Job* by Richard T. Wright and Scott Decker. This was a 1994 survey in St. Louis of 105 currently active burglars. The authors observed, "One of the most serious risks faced by residential burglars is the possibility of being injured or killed by occupants of a target. Many of the offenders we spoke to reported that this was far and away their greatest fear."

The fear of armed victims is not limited to the home. Unlike most other nations, America allows its citizens to be armed for protection not only in their home but in their place of business. A 1996 study of 310 armed robbers, by Athena Research in Seattle, reported that many robbers are afraid of armed victims more than anything else. The fear of armed victims is why armed robbers often avoid "mom and pop" stores where the victim may be armed. Instead, robbers concentrate on chain stores, where corporate policy frequently forbids employees to be armed.

Real-world experiments yield results consistent with burglars' reports of their desire to avoid confrontations with armed victims. In the 1960's, gun control advocates in New York City handed out window decals, so that homeowners could proclaim that their home did not contain a gun.

The decals quickly became a magnet for burglars, and the decal program was abandoned. The converse of the New York City "victimize this house" program are the real-world experiments in which cities have forcefully reminded potential burglars of the dangers of armed victims.

Gun ownership as a warning to criminals

In Orlando in 1967, the police responded to a rape epidemic by initiating a highly publicized program training women in firearms use. While rape increased in the nation and in Florida over the next year, the rape rate fell 88 percent in Orlando, and burglary dropped 22 percent. The same year, rising rates of store robberies prompted a similar (but smaller-scale) program in Kansas City, Missouri, to train store owners in gun use. The next year, while the robbery rate in Missouri and the United States continued to rise significantly, the rate fell in the Kansas City metro area. The trend of increasing burglary in the area also came to an abrupt end, contrary to state and national patterns.

In 1982, the town of Kennesaw, Georgia, horrified the national media by passing an ordinance requiring every home to have a gun. (Exceptions were made for conscientious objectors, people with criminal records, and various other categories.) In the seven months before the ordinance, there had been 45 residential burglaries. In the seven months after the ordinance, there were only five—an 89 percent decline. Over the next five years, the residential burglary rate in Kennesaw was 85 percent below the rate before the enactment of the ordinance.

The ordinance may not have actually changed gun ownership patterns much in Kennesaw; the mayor estimated that even before the ordinance, about five of every six Kennesaw homes contained a gun. But the publicity surrounding the Kennesaw law may have served as a very powerful warning to persons contemplating a residential burglary in the town: any homeowner confronted during a burglary would almost certainly be armed.

Not just in Kennesaw, but throughout the United States, the armed victim is a serious danger to burglars. One of 31 burglars has been shot during a burglary. Thus, American burglary patterns are heavily influenced by the perpetrators' fears of confronting an armed victim. Most burglars report that they avoid late-night burglaries because "That's the way to get shot."

Gun ownership for home protection is considerably more beneficial to the entire community than many other anti-burglary measures.

Opponents of gun ownership for home defense insist that—despite what burglars say again and again—the fear of armed victims has little to do with burglary patterns. Instead, burglars are claimed to be nonconfrontational by nature, wanting to avoid seeing any victim, armed or not. But this assertion fails to explain why burglars in Great Britain or Canada are so much less shy than their American cousins. Besides, burglars are *not* nonconfrontational by nature. A multistate study of felony prisoners found that 62 percent of burglars had also perpetrated robberies. (A burglary is an entry into a building to commit a felony, and does not necessarily involve a confrontation; a robbery is the taking of property from a victim through force or the threat of force.)

The St. Louis study of currently active burglars observed: "Most offenders in our sample . . . showed little concern for the well-being of their victims. In fact, several of them said they were prepared to use violence against anyone who got in their way during the commission of an offense." As one St. Louis burglar told Wright and Decker: "When [the victims] come in there, they better have some boxin' gloves on cause . . . I'm gon hurt you, I ain't lyin'."

When victims cannot protect themselves

When burglars do encounter victims who cannot protect themselves, the results can be terrifying. In 30 percent of the cases in which a burglar does confront a victim, the victim is assaulted or threatened. In ten percent of these cases, the assaults turn into rapes. Florida State University criminologist Gary Kleck, in *Point Blank: Guns and Violence in America*, explains the implications of these statistics:

> Suppose that the percentage of "hot" burglaries rose from current American levels (around 12 or 13%) to the Canadian level (around 45%). Knowing how often a hot burglary turns into an assault, we can predict that an increase in hot burglaries to Canadian levels would result in 545,713 more assaults every year. This by itself would raise the American violent crime rate 9.4%.

While the gun prohibition lobby portrays gun owners as atavistic and selfish, gun ownership for home protection is considerably more beneficial to the entire community than many other anti-burglary measures.

In responsible hands, guns are no danger at all, since the gun will only shoot in the direction in which it is pointed.

Burglars (or convenience-store robbers) do not know which of their potential victims may be armed. Until a confrontation with a homeowner, the potential burglar generally has no idea whether any given homeowner has a gun. Thus, burglars must (and most do) take care to avoid entering any home where a victim might be present. Because about half of all American homes contain a gun, burglars tend to avoid all occupied American homes. People who don't own guns—even people who belong to gun-prohibition organizations—enjoy free-rider safety benefits from America's armed homes.

In contrast to guns, burglar alarms appear to have no net community benefit. Burglar alarms have been shown to reduce burglaries for homes in which they are installed; but the presence of many burglar alarms in a neighborhood does not appear to decrease or increase the burglary rate for unalarmed homes.

False alarms—which account for 94 to 98 [percent] of all burglar alarm activations—impose very large public safety costs through misappropriation of limited police resources. False-alarm signals travel over 911 lines, and may crowd out genuine emergencies. Guns, of course, lie inert until someone decides to use them; they do not go off because a cat jumped into a beam of light.

Gun prohibitionists make all sorts of claims about the risks of "a gun in the home," and these claims have some validity if the gun happens to be in the home of a violet felon, or an alcoholic, or a person with suicidal tendencies. But in responsible hands, guns are no danger at all, since the gun will only shoot in the direction in which it is pointed, and will not fire unless the trigger is pulled.

The benefits provided by guns

In any case, whatever risks a gun in the home may present are borne almost entirely by the people in that home. The non-gunowners in the community get the benefit of safety from home-invasion burglars, while assuming no risks at all. (The only significant external danger of a gun in the home is if the gun is stolen by a criminal, a risk that also applies to any other device that could be stolen and used by a criminal, such as a car or a crowbar, or any valuables which could be sold and the profits used to buy crime tools.) And, of course, guns stay quiet and unobtrusive until needed. They do not bark all night and wake up the neighborhood, like dogs often do. Nor do guns rush into the street to attack and sometimes kill innocent people, as some guard dogs do. Guns in the right hands do nothing at all, until they are needed. Firearms, which are typically stored deep inside a home, do not make a neighborhood look ugly. But window bars give a neighborhood the appearance of a prison, and some window bars can trap the occupants of a home during a fire.

Most people consider it rational for householders to have burglary insurance. Yet insurance premiums must (for the insurance company to stay in business) be set at a level at which the cost of the premiums exceeds the probable payout by the insurance company over the long run. Insurance is, by definition, a losing bet. If it is reasonable for people to reduce the risks of burglary by buying insurance, it is far more reasonable for people to reduce the risks of burglary by purchasing a gun for home protection. Over a ten-year period, the cost of insurance premiums far exceeds the cost of a good gun. Moreover, the gun, unlike the insurance premium, can actually prevent a victim from being injured.

The antigun lobby

Unfortunately, the antigun lobby is morally opposed to gun ownership for defensive purposes. As Sarah Brady explains, "To me, the only reason for guns in civilian hands is for sporting purposes." This view is antithetical to legislation enacted in Colorado and other states which makes explicit the common-law right to use deadly force against violent home invaders. Thus, the antigun lobbies push for laws like Canada's, which effectively abolishes home defense. In Canada, "safe storage" laws require that guns be stored unloaded or locked up, thus making them difficult to deploy in a sudden emergency. The antigun lobbies and their numerous media allies are also running a propaganda campaign against guns in the home—a campaign which tries to convince ordinary Americans that they are just as prone to criminal violence as are convicted felons and substance abusers. But as long as tens of millions of Americans continue to exercise their constitutional right to own a gun to protect their homes and families, then all Americans will continue to enjoy lower risks of assault and greater safety in their homes, thanks to the widespread community benefits of guns in the right hands.

3

Gun Control Can Reduce Crime

Douglas Weil

Douglas Weil is the director of research at the Center to Prevent Handgun Violence in Washington, D.C.

Research asserting that gun ownership reduces crime is flawed. Government surveys, which are far more comprehensive than other studies, show that using guns for protection is less common than believed and that the rate of robbery—the most common crime between strangers on the street—differs little among states that permit their residents to carry concealed weapons and those that do not. Other research has found that gun homicides and suicides decline when access to guns is restricted. Strict gun control laws would reduce the supply of guns to criminals and should be enacted. Moreover, the gun industry must start to take responsibility for its products' contribution to society's problems.

Over the past few years, many state legislatures have debated, and a significant number have passed, legislation that eases restrictions on carrying concealed handguns. At the heart of this effort is the belief that "encouraging gun ownership might be a partial solution to the crime problem."

An increased risk of injury

The evidence that crime reduction can be achieved through the proliferation of gun ownership and gun carrying is weak, and the strategy is dangerous because it is based on the false premise that acquiring a firearm for protection will, in general, make people safer. In support of a petition before the Federal Trade Commission, seventy-five nationally recognized researchers and other health professionals wrote that advertising suggesting that the purchase of a handgun will increase the security and safety of the consumer is "at odds with the best available epidemiologic evidence." The letter continues that "bringing a gun, especially a handgun, into the

From Douglas Weil, "Gun Control Laws Can Reduce Crime." This article first appeared in the February 1997 issue, and is reprinted by permission of, *The World and I*, a publication of The Washington Times Corporation. Copyright ©1997.

home for self-protection will, on average, increase the risk of a homicide, suicide, and unintentional injury occurring in the home. The increased risk of fatal injury is borne almost entirely by the gun owner and his or her family and friends."

There is, of course, a sensible alternative to those who envision America as a place in which the citizenry is responsible for combating crime by arming itself. The alternative is to: (1) put into place a well-tailored, comprehensive set of gun control measures designed to disrupt the illegal trafficking and distribution of firearms, and (2) apply appropriate pressure to the gun industry to ensure that the design and marketing strategies for firearms that are brought to the market minimize the potential for criminal use of guns while respecting the legitimate use of these weapons.

The evidence that crime reduction can be achieved through the proliferation of gun ownership and gun carrying is weak.

The use of a gun for protection is an incredibly rare event—a fact that simply won't change if more people are "armed and dangerous." But bringing more guns into homes—where married couples occasionally fight, in which teens sometimes contemplate suicide, and in which the curiosity of young children often leads them to look through their parents' dresser drawers—will lead to more death. Rather than enabling their citizens to carry concealed guns into movie theaters, shopping malls, and grocery stores, other industrialized nations have enacted laws that curb the supply of handguns to criminals and other individuals who pose a high risk to society. In 1992, there were 13,220 handgun murders in the United States; Great Britain had 33. Isn't it obvious that there is a better way?

Faulty research perpetuates myths

The case for gun ownership and gun carrying as a crime reduction strategy is based on conclusions drawn from two pieces of research: Gary Kleck's long-standing claim that use of guns for protection is common, and John Lott and David Mustard's more recent claim that allowing individuals to carry concealed handguns deters violent crime. Upon close inspection, however, this research has obvious flaws.

Twice each year, the federal government obtains data on the frequency, characteristics, and consequences of criminal victimization from a nationally representative sample of fifty thousand households that participate in the National Crime Victimization Survey. It is the best available data on criminal victimization in the country. Researchers at the University of Maryland analyzed these data and concluded that "criminals face little threat from armed victims." Though the researchers estimated that victims use firearms for protection approximately sixty-five thousand times a year, they concluded that when "coupled with the risks of keeping a gun in the home for protection, these results raise questions about the collective benefits of civilian firearm ownership for crime control."

For his study, Kleck surveyed just five thousand individuals. He asked each person if he had used a firearm in self-defense and, if he had done so, under what circumstance and with what effect. His conclusion—which is based on only 53 reported incidents—is that guns are used for protection 2.5 million times. This figure—more than thirty times greater than estimates derived from the much larger National Crime Victimization Survey—is easily dismissed when put in context with other findings from Kleck's research that bear no resemblance to what we know about the real world.

According to Kleck's survey, women defend themselves with a firearm in 40 percent of all sexual assaults—even though we know that guns are rarely used in these circumstances. In fact, a firearm is used for protection in the case of sexual assault in fewer than one in a hundred incidents. Also according to Kleck's data, a firearm is used for protection in 80 percent of the instances of burglary when a victim is at home (including those people who are asleep)—despite the fact that only 40 percent of all households have a firearm. For this finding to be true, burglars must have an uncanny knack of victimizing only households in which the owner has a gun. Even more confusing is Kleck's finding that victims shoot (wounding or killing) an assailant over 190,000 times a year. This is simply not possible. The total number of people who are shot under all circumstances each year (including suicide, homicide, and unintentional shootings) is less than 190,000 incidents. These findings from Kleck's survey clearly undermine any claims he might make about the use of a gun in self-defense.

Lott and Mustard's research findings on the impact on crime of allowing people to carry concealed handguns are also puzzling. The researchers came to two principal conclusions: (1) that allowing citizens to carry concealed handguns deters rape, murder, and aggravated assault—though they find little or no evidence that concealed handguns deters robbers, and (2) that criminals who stopped committing rapes, murders, and aggravated assaults did not give up crime—rather, they started committing more crimes that minimized the risk of interpersonal contact (e.g., auto theft and larceny). Upon close examination, these findings are difficult to understand. For example, does anyone really believe that auto theft is a substitute for rape and murder?

Criminals face little threat from armed victims.

More to the point, if carrying a concealed handgun were going to have a beneficial impact on crime, the deterrent effect would, presumably, be related to predatory crimes between strangers that occur on the street. Consequently, easing restrictions on the carrying of concealed weapons should have the biggest impact on robbery. Fewer than one in five murders occur in connection with a predatory crime, and the majority of rapes and aggravated assaults occur between people who know each other—and they often occur in the home. Robbery typically occurs on the street and between strangers. But Lott and Mustard are hard pressed to find any impact of carrying concealed weapons on robbery. The only explanation is that their study is fundamentally flawed.

Other researchers have concluded that there is no beneficial impact on crime associated with easing restrictions on carrying concealed handguns. In fact, in a study of five large urban areas, researchers at the University of Maryland concluded that easing restrictions on carrying concealed weapons was associated with an increase in gun-related murders that was not offset by a decrease in murders committed with other weapons. The researchers hypothesized that criminals responded to the change in the law by arming themselves more frequently, doing so with more powerful weapons, and being quicker to use their guns during the commission of a crime.

Gun laws work

There is little published research on the effectiveness of gun laws, though with little dissent most of the studies that do exist support the notion that well-tailored gun laws can have a beneficial impact on gun violence, while laws that indiscriminately increase access to firearms may have the opposite effect. For example, researchers found a "prompt decline in homicides and suicides by firearms in the District of Columbia" following implementation of a restrictive licensing law for handguns in the District. Conversely, the evidence from the five urban areas studied suggests that relaxing restrictions on carrying concealed firearms led to an increase in gun homicides.

Researchers have also shown that we have effective strategies for disrupting the illegal interstate trafficking of firearms. In July 1993, Virginia became the second state in the nation to limit handgun purchases by individuals to one gun a month (though gun collectors can obtain permission to exceed the legal limit). Prior to the enactment of the law, individuals were able to purchase an unlimited number of handguns from licensed dealers as part of a single transaction. The law was passed because Virginia was a principal supplier of guns to the illegal market, particularly to the northeastern part of the United States. In fact, prior to the law, 35 percent of all guns that were originally obtained in the Southeast and then illegally trafficked to New York, New Jersey, Connecticut, Rhode Island, or Massachusetts came from Virginia. Shortly after the law took effect, the percentage of guns that were being trafficked to the Northeast from Virginia fell to only 16 percent.

Well-tailored gun laws can have a beneficial impact on gun violence.

The truth is that crime and the violent outcomes associated with criminal activity are affected by a variety of factors, and society's response cannot be monolithic or simplistic. Part of the solution is implementation of a comprehensive set of well-tailored gun laws directed at keeping guns out of the illegal market. In 1993, 1.1 million violent crimes were committed with handguns—many of which were acquired in the illegal market. In fact, when asked, approximately 30 to 43 percent of criminals identify the illegal market as the source of their last handgun.

The illegal market exists for a variety of reasons. Would-be criminals may be unable to buy handguns from the legal market, because a prior criminal record disqualifies them from legally purchasing the weapons. To date, because of the Brady Law more than 100,000 prohibited purchasers (including 72,000 felons) were denied access to a handgun that they attempted to purchase from a gun dealer. Others may go to the illegal market because they want to make it difficult for law enforcement to trace a gun back to them—something that can also be accomplished by purchasing a gun from the private or secondary market (transactions that do not involve a licensed gun dealer). The ability to acquire guns from the illegal or the secondary market points to one of the most troubling aspects of society's attempts to prevent gun violence—the ease with which the link between a gun and the individual who uses it can be broken, removing an important impediment to the criminal use of firearms.

In many jurisdictions, identification requirements for the purchase of a firearm are minimal and easily falsified, while private or secondary market sales are largely unregulated. A prohibited purchaser or individual who, for any reason, does not want to be identified as the owner of a particular gun can obtain a firearm directly from the secondary market with little risk of being stopped or identified. Alternatively, the same individual could recruit a third party (known as a "straw purchaser") to buy the gun in his place. If a gun bought by a straw purchaser turns up as part of a criminal investigation, the straw purchaser can, with little risk of criminal culpability, claim that he sold the firearm to an unidentifiable third party.

Requiring individuals to obtain a license prior to purchasing a firearm will make it more difficult to purchase a gun using false identification.

To make it more difficult to break the link between a gun and the individual who uses it—and therefore to reduce the supply of guns available to criminals, several steps can be taken:

• individuals should be required to obtain a license (or "permit-to-purchase") before being allowed to buy a gun, particularly a handgun. The license should be issued only after the applicant provides proof of residency and submits to a fingerprint-based background check;

• all handgun transfers (if not all firearms transfers) should be registered;

• laws that regulate the purchase of a firearm from a licensed gun dealer should be extended to private, secondary market transactions; and

• handgun purchases should be limited to one gun every thirty days.

Taken together, these measures will make it more difficult for gun traffickers to supply the illegal market with firearms. Also, requiring individuals to obtain a license prior to purchasing a firearm will make it more difficult to purchase a gun using false identification. As a result, there will be a greater need for individuals who do not want their names associated with the purchase of a gun to seek out straw purchasers to buy the gun for them, though recruiting straw purchasers should be more difficult. Fewer individuals would be willing to act as straw purchasers if they were required to submit their names to law enforcement for a background check to buy a gun that they intend to illegally transfer to a third party.

Requiring that all firearms transfers be registered, including those in the private market, would likely further complicate the process of recruiting straw purchasers. If all transfers are registered, then the most recent owner of a gun recovered as part of a criminal investigation can be easily identified, and when asked, that individual will not be free to say that he passed the gun on to an unidentifiable third party. Because registration has the potential to make it difficult for an individual to break the link between his possession and use of a firearm, the California Police Chiefs Association has called for registration of all handgun transfers.

During the 1996 legislative session in Maryland, the state legislature considered a comprehensive package of measures proposed by Gov. Parris Glendening to regulate private gun ownership. A requirement that prospective purchasers obtain a license prior to acquiring a handgun was one element of the package. The Center to Prevent Handgun Violence attempted to assess the efficacy of the licensing requirement by comparing the use of a firearm in violent crime and in suicide in New Jersey—where a license must be obtained before an individual can purchase a handgun—and in Maryland. Our analysis of the data suggests that licensing may reduce the use of firearms in crime and suicide.

The gun industry needs to take responsibility

Well-tailored gun laws should be a part of society's response to crime and the violence associated with criminal activity, but it should not be the only response. The gun industry, through its own actions in the development of products it brings to the market, contributes to the problems society faces. Consequently, the industry should be pressured to take responsibility for its contribution to the problem in the hope that it can be part of the solution.

The gun industry manufactures and markets the only widely available consumer products designed to kill. As designed, however, most guns can be fired by virtually anyone who gains access to them—whether a three-year-old child or an unauthorized adult who steals a gun and then uses it to commit other crimes. But guns could be designed differently. Readily available technology exists that can be used to "personalize" guns so that they can be fired only by authorized users. The industry, however, has failed to incorporate this technology into the design of its products while producing an endless stream of products better suited to criminal purposes than legitimate use.

Gun manufacturers, for example, have brought to the market assault pistols that accept silencers and high-capacity ammunition magazines along with low-quality, easily concealable Saturday Night Specials. More recently, the industry has developed ever smaller versions of its high-powered 9mm semiautomatic pistols. Without a doubt, the gun industry is able to innovate new designs of its lethal products—it just chooses to innovate for death and injury rather than for safety. Like the tobacco industry, the gun industry must accept the burden of responsibility for preventing the criminal and violent outcomes associated with the use of the products they design and sell.

A number of myths are associated with gun control. One of these myths is that gun laws burden only the law-abiding citizen. Another myth is that gun laws do not work—or more specifically, that they cannot be used to keep guns out of the hands of criminals. But these are clearly myths, and the longer they are kept alive, the more difficult it is to make rational decisions about the proper role of gun control in the broader effort to reduce the amount of crime and criminal violence that occurs in the United States.

We need to implement a comprehensive set of gun laws designed to limit the number of guns available to criminals.

We know that well-tailored gun laws work. The Brady Law is working to prevent easy access to handguns by criminals. Since the law was first implemented, eighty-five felons a day have been denied access to a handgun that they tried to purchase from licensed gun dealers. Virginia's law limiting handgun purchases to one gun a month has had an enormous impact on gun trafficking patterns along the East Coast. This law should be extended to cover handgun purchases in all states. Who besides gun traffickers need to be allowed to purchase more than one handgun every thirty days?

Most gun control policies currently advocated in the United States (e.g., licensing, registration, regulation of secondary market sales, and one gun a month) could be best described as efforts to limit the supply of guns to the illegal market, and the tools necessary to maintain the link between the guns that are used for illegal purposes and the criminals who have used them. And they should be part of a rational strategy to reduce gun violence in America.

The gun lobby believes an armed society is a polite society—"much social order in America may depend on the fact that millions of people are armed and dangerous to each other." Well, America is an armed society (a firearm can be found in 40 percent of all households in the United States), but it is difficult to say that our tremendous firepower has made us safe.

It is time to try a better way. It is time to make a serious effort to keep guns out of the hands of criminals. And it is time for the gun industry to become a partner in the effort to reduce the level of violence caused by the products it brings to the market. We need to implement a comprehensive set of gun laws designed to limit the number of guns available to criminals.

4

Gun Control Does Not Reduce Crime

John R. Lott Jr.

John R. Lott Jr. is the John M. Olin law and economics professor at the University of Chicago School of Law and the author of More Guns, Less Crime: Understanding Crime and Gun Control Laws.

The political response after every tragedy involving guns is to pass more laws restricting access to guns. However, it is unlikely that one more law will succeed where twenty thousand other federal and state laws have failed. Guns are used far more frequently to prevent a crime than to commit a crime. Restrictive gun laws make law-abiding citizens much more vulnerable to criminals and are more likely to lead to the loss of innocent lives than to save lives.

Keeping their promise to President Clinton, Republican leaders in Congress have moved quickly to consider a broad range of gun-control laws in the wake of the Littleton, Colorado, attack [in which two teenage boys shot and killed twelve students at Columbine High School in April 1999]. The Senate will be debating and voting on a range of new proposals, with the House Judiciary Committee set to start hearings. Mr. Clinton says that we must "do something" and that he knows "one thing for certain": If more restrictions had been enacted, "there would have been fewer kids killed."

But would more gun laws save lives? There are already a large number of laws in place. The Columbine murderers, Eric Harris and Dylan Klebold, violated at least 17 state and federal weapons-control laws. Mark E. Manes, who allegedly sold the handgun to Harris and Klebold, may have violated at least one federal and one state law, and if either of the killers' parents knew their child possessed a handgun, they would have run afoul of a Colorado law. Nationwide there are more than 20,000 gun-control laws that regulate everything from who can own a gun and how it can be purchased to where one can possess or use it.

Costs and benefits

Regulations have both costs and benefits, and rules that are passed to solve a problem can sometimes make it worse. The biggest problem with gun-control laws is that those who are intent on harming others, and especially those who plan to commit suicide, are the least likely to obey them. Mr. Clinton frames the issue in terms of whether hunters are willing to be "inconvenienced," but this misses the real question: Will well-intended laws disarm potential victims and thus make it easier for criminals? Potential victims use guns more than two million times a year to stop violent crimes; 98% of the time simply brandishing a gun is sufficient to stop an attack. Crimes are stopped with guns about five times as frequently as crimes are committed with guns.

The biggest problem with gun-control laws is that those who are intent on harming others . . . are the least likely to obey them.

Consider, then, the costs and benefits of Mr. Clinton's main proposals:
• *Waiting periods.* A three-day waiting period for handgun purchases could not possibly have stopped the Littleton attack, which the killers had been planning for a year. Mr. Clinton focuses on the general benefits from a "cooling-off period," and such benefits might exist. Yet real drawbacks exist, too. Those threatened with harm may not be able to quickly obtain a gun for protection. Experience with the Brady waiting period that lapsed last year, as well as with state waiting periods, indicates that these laws are either neutral or do more harm than good. In the only academic research done on the Brady law, I found that the national waiting period had no significant impact on murder or robbery rates and was associated with a small increase in rape and aggravated-assault rates.
• *Mandatory gun locks.* This proposal, too, is unrelated to the attack in Colorado; Eric Harris and Dylan Klebold would have known how to unlock their guns. Mr. Clinton claims that gun locks will save lives, particularly those of young children. In 1996, 30 children under five died in gun accidents—fewer than the number who died of drowning in water buckets. With some 80 million Americans owning 240 million guns, the vast majority of gun owners must be extremely careful or such accidents would be much more frequent.

More important, thousands of children are protected each year by parents or other adults using guns to defend themselves and their families. Mechanical locks that fit either into a gun's barrel or over its trigger require the gun to be unloaded; and locked, unloaded guns offer far less protection from intruders. Thus requiring locks would surely increase deaths resulting from crime. Gun locks may make sense for parents who live in low-crime areas, but this should be a matter of individual choice.
• *Prison sentences for adults whose guns are misused by someone under 18.* Parents are already civilly liable for wrongful actions committed by their children, but Mr. Clinton proposes a three-year minimum prison term for anyone whose gun is used improperly by any minor, regardless of

whether the gun owner consents to or knows of the use. This is draconian, to say the least, the equivalent of sending Mom and Dad to prison because an auto thief kills someone while driving the family car.

• *New rules for gun shows.* The Clinton administration has provided no evidence that such shows are important in supplying criminals with guns. What's more, it is simply false to claim that the rules for purchasing guns at a gun show are any different from those regarding gun purchases anywhere else. Dealers who sell guns at a show must perform the same background checks and obey all the other rules that they do when they make sales at their stores. Private sales are unregulated whether they occur at a gun show or not.

If, as Mr. Clinton proposes, the government enacts new laws regulating private sales at gun shows, all someone would have to do is walk outside the show and sell the gun there. To regulate private sales, the government would have to register all guns. Those who advocate the new rules for gun shows should be willing to acknowledge openly if their real goal is registration.

• *Age limits.* Mr. Clinton proposes a federal ban on possession of handguns by anyone under 21. Under a 1968 federal law, 21 is already the minimum age to purchase a handgun, but setting the age to possess a handgun is a state matter. While some people between 18 and 21 use guns improperly, others face the risk of crime and would benefit from defending themselves. My own research indicates that laws allowing those between 18 and 21 years of age to carry a concealed handgun reduce violent crimes just as well as those limited to citizens over 21.

• *Background checks for purchasers of bomb-making material.* This will have little effect, simply because few items are likely to be covered. No one seriously discusses including fertilizer, used to make the bomb that killed 168 in Oklahoma City in 1995, or propane tanks like the ones found after the Littleton massacre. There are simply too many common household items that can be used to make bombs.

Regard for facts

Much of the debate over gun control these days is conducted without regard for facts. For example, the press reproduces pictures of a Tech-9, the so-called assault pistol used in the Columbine attack. The pictures show a much larger ammunition clip than was actually used, making it look as frightening as possible. Few reports even mention that at most one of the 13 Littleton victims was killed with this gun. In spite of all the rhetoric and despite its appearance, this "assault weapon" functions no differently from other semiautomatic pistols sold in the U.S. It is no more powerful, it doesn't shoot any faster, and it doesn't shoot any more rounds. One pull of the trigger fires one bullet.

Good intentions don't necessarily make good laws. What counts is whether the laws will ultimately save lives. The real tragedy of Mr. Clinton's proposals is that they are likely to lead to the loss of more lives.

5

Carrying Concealed Weapons Reduces Crime

Morgan Reynolds and H. Sterling Burnett

Morgan Reynolds is the director of the National Center for Policy Analysis (NCPA) Criminal Justice Center. H. Sterling Burnett is a policy analyst with the NCPA, a public policy institute that analyzes and debates research on national issues.

Because the Supreme Court has ruled that the police are not obligated to protect citizens from crime, individuals must be responsible for their own protection. Carrying a concealed weapon is one way people can protect themselves against crime. States that permit their residents to carry a concealed weapon have reduced their murder, rape, and assault rates because criminals are more wary of attacking potentially armed citizens. Furthermore, studies have found very few incidents of criminal behavior or accidental firings by concealed-weapons permit holders.

Since 1986 the number of states in which it is legal to carry concealed weapons has grown from nine to 31, representing 49 percent of the country's population. Should we feel safer?

Opponents of right-to-carry laws predicted a sharp decline in public safety because minor incidents would escalate into killings and more children would be victimized by more guns in irresponsible hands. Further, critics claimed that criminals would be undeterred by any increase in armed citizens. Indeed, they claimed that right-to-carry laws would increase crime rather than deter it. Experience has proven them wrong.

Objections

What objections do the critics offer?

Objection #1: Citizens are safe enough without handguns.

Criminals commit 10 million violent and 30 million property crimes a year. Hospital emergency rooms treat an estimated 1.4 million people a

Reprinted from Morgan Reynolds and H. Sterling Burnett, "No Smoking Guns: Answering Objections to Right-to-Carry Laws," *NCPA Brief Analysis*, no. 246, November 17, 1997, with permission.

year for injuries inflicted in violent attacks, according to a recent Department of Justice study.

Since the U.S. Supreme Court and lower courts have held that the police are not obligated to protect individuals from crime, citizens are ultimately responsible for their own defense. Carrying a handgun allows millions to effectively provide for their own protection.

Carrying a handgun allows millions to effectively provide for their own protection.

Objection #2: Concealed weapons do not deter crime.

In choosing their crimes, criminals weigh the prospective costs against the benefits. If criminals suspect that the costs will be too high, they are less likely to commit a crime. The possibility of a concealed weapon tilts the odds against the criminal and in favor of the victim. A survey of 1,847 felons in 10 states found them more concerned about meeting an armed victim than running into the police.

Their concern is well founded. Victims use handguns an estimated 1.9 million times each year in self-defense against an attack by another person, according to a survey conducted by Florida State University criminologist Gary Kleck. Studies have found that robbery and rape victims who resist with a gun cut the risks of injury in half.

Moreover, a study by economists John Lott and David Mustard of the University of Chicago, published in the January 1997 *Journal of Legal Studies*, examined the impact of concealed carry permits. Using data from all 3,054 U.S. counties between 1977 and 1992, the study found that:

- Concealed handgun laws reduced murder by 8.5 percent, rape by 5 percent and severe assault by 7 percent.
- Had right-to-carry prevailed throughout the country, 1,600 fewer murders, 4,200 fewer rapes and 60,000 fewer severe assaults would have occurred during those 15 years.

In addition, the deterrent effect of concealed handgun laws proved highest in counties with high crime rates. For example, FBI statistics showed that in counties with populations of more than 200,000 (typically the counties with the highest rates of violent crime), laws allowing concealed carry produced a 13 percent drop in the murder rate and a 7 percent decline in rapes.

Case study: Vermont

Vermont has long had the least restrictive firearms carry laws, allowing citizens to carry guns either openly or concealed without any permit. Vermont also has maintained one of the lowest violent crime rates in the country. For example:

- In 1980, when murders and robberies in the U.S. had soared to an average of 10 and 251 per 100,000 population, respectively, Vermont's murder rate was 22 percent of the national rate and its robbery rate was 15 percent.
- In 1996 Vermont's rates remained among the lowest in the coun-

try at 25 percent of the national rate for homicide and 8 percent for robbery.

Objection #3: Right-to-carry laws boost killings on impulse.

Widespread gun availability was supposed to lead to a "wild-west" mentality with more shootings and deaths as people vented their anger with pistols instead of fists. Yet FBI data show that, as a share of all homicides, killings that resulted from arguments declined. In addition:

- Dade County, Florida, kept meticulous records for six years, and of 21,000 permit holders, none was known to have injured an innocent person.
- Since Virginia passed a right-to-carry law, more than 50,000 permits have been issued, not one permit holder has been convicted of a crime and violent crime has dropped.

Moreover, those who have broken the rules have lost their privilege to carry a gun.

- Texas has revoked or suspended nearly 300 permits for minor violations like failure to conceal or carrying a gun in a bar.
- Between 1987 and 1995, Florida issued nearly 300,000 permits, but revoked only 19 because the permit holder had committed a crime. That's one crime per 14,000 permit holders during a nine-year period, an incredibly low rate compared to a criminal arrest rate of one per 14 Americans age 15 and older each year.

Concealed handgun laws reduced murder by 8.5 percent, rape by 5 percent and severe assault by 7 percent.

Objection #4: Concealed carry puts guns in untrained hands.

Before issuing a concealed carry permit, most states require that the applicant prove he or she has been thoroughly trained, with:

- 10 to 15 hours emphasizing conflict resolution.
- A pre-test and a final test covering the laws of self-defense and the consequences of misuse of deadly force.
- A stress on gun safety in the classroom and on the firing range.
- A stringent shooting accuracy test which applicants must pass each time they renew their permit.

Of course, a person who has only a split second to decide whether to use deadly force can make a mistake. However, only about 30 such mistaken civilian shootings occur nationwide each year. The police kill in error three times as often.

Objection #5: Concealed carry increases accidental gun deaths.

The Lott-Mustard study found no increase in accidental shootings in counties with "shall issue" right-to-carry laws, where authorities have to issue the permit to all who meet the criteria. Nor have other studies. Nationally, there are about 1,400 accidental firearms deaths each year—far fewer than the number of deaths attributable to medical errors or automobile accidents. The national death rate from firearms has declined even while firearm ownership has almost doubled in the last 20 years, and 22 more states have liberalized right-to-carry laws:

- The fatal firearm accident rate has declined to about .5 per 100,000 people—a decrease of more than 19 percent in the last decade.
- The number of fatal firearms-related accidents among children fell to an all-time low of 185 in 1994, a 64 percent decline since 1975.

A social good

Concealed carry laws have not contributed to a big increase in gun ownership. Nor has allowing citizens the right to carry firearms for self-protection led to the negative consequences claimed by critics. In fact, these laws have lowered violent crime rates and increased the general level of knowledge concerning the rights, responsibilities and laws of firearm ownership.

Putting unarmed citizens at the mercy of armed and violent criminals was never a good idea. Now that the evidence is in, we know that concealed carry is a social good.

6

The Research on Concealed Weapons Laws Is Flawed

Franklin Zimring and Gordon Hawkins

Franklin Zimring is the director of the Earl Warren Legal Institute at the University of California at Berkeley. Gordon Hawkins is a fellow at the Earl Warren Legal Institute. They are the authors of Crime Is Not the Problem: Lethal Violence in America.

A study quoted extensively by the antigun control lobby claims that permitting individuals to carry concealed weapons would prevent thousands of murders, rapes, and assaults each year. However, the study's claims are based on problematic methodology, models, and conclusions. The study concludes that laws allowing concealed weapons reduce crime without examining whether these laws lead to an increased number of people carrying firearms and using them to prevent crime, or whether the carrying of concealed weapons deters criminal behavior. Furthermore, subsequent examination of the data by other researchers has yielded different conclusions. The only policy that will reduce lethal violence in the United States is one that reduces the number of guns in society.

There is a new wrinkle this season in the tired debate about gun control in the United States. A statistical analysis has been released with the flamboyantly specific claim that relaxing the remaining restrictions on concealed handguns in the United States would prevent "approximately 1,570 murders, 4,177 rapes, and over 60,000 assaults" each year. According to the study's authors, John R. Lott Jr. and David B. Mustard, the "estimated annual gain from allowing concealed handguns is at least $6.214 billion." This estimate was based on a multivariate regression analysis that showed lower murder and crime rates in jurisdictions that had made it easier for citizens to obtain permits to carry concealed firearms on their persons and in cars.

This new "right to carry" study is newsworthy in three respects. First, the crime prevention claims are very large and yet the legal changes nec-

Reprinted from Franklin Zimring and Gordon Hawkins, "Concealed Handguns: The Counterfeit Deterrent," *The Responsive Community*, Spring 1997, with permission.

essary to achieve them are modest and do not involve financial costs. Here lies the promise of crime control on the cheap. Second, the people making these claims are not from the local branch of the National Rifle Association. The study is authored by a postdoctoral fellow in law and economics and a graduate economics student at the University of Chicago. Any connection of research to a reputable institution of higher learning is worthy of notice in a field where so many "studies" are transparent special pleading.

Third, from the perspective of a television news producer, the most exciting aspect of this new study is the method by which the legal changes are supposed to save lives and reduce crime. Whereas most observers worry that the city streets of the United States have too many people carrying guns on them, this new study announces that increasing the number of loaded handguns on our streets will reduce the number of citizens killed and wounded. This is what newspaper editors in bygone days used to call a "man bites dog" story. What could be more paradoxical than asserting that the current violence problem could be ameliorated by more guns rather than fewer?

The distinctive problem in the United States is not rates of crime, but rather high rates of lethal violence.

Released to the press five months prior to its publication in January 1997, this new analysis of right-to-carry laws is becoming a discrete chapter in the debate about American policy toward guns and violence. The Lott and Mustard claims are of special interest to this journal's audience for two reasons. First, the substantive question of whether more guns or fewer is the appropriate path to safer communities is of obvious importance. Second, the data and methods encountered in this study are typical of a genre of studies using multiple regression techniques to support statements about the effects of government policy. Are these reliable methods of determining the impact of government policy? What are the limits of the methodology? For communities to have reasonable dialogues about issues of importance—and given that people will often turn to "experts" for analysis—these questions are of more than just theoretical importance. Thus one goal of this essay is to make the seemingly arcane world of econometric models more accessible.

This essay will tell the "right-to-carry" story in four brief installments. We will first describe how state laws dealing with carrying concealed firearms became an important part of the politics of gun control in the 1980s, and how state level politics determined which states passed the National Rifle Association–sponsored legal changes. Those demographic factors are crucial to evaluating the validity of Lott and Mustard. Having described the origins of the legal changes, we will then turn our attention to the data assembled by Lott and Mustard to evaluate the impact of right-to-carry laws. The third section describes some of the statistical materials that have been put forward by critics of the Lott and Mustard study, materials that cast doubt on the causal relation Lott and Mustard advance.

The final section contrasts the debate about concealed weapons laws with the accumulating evidence on the influence of gun use on rates of violence in the United States. While one problem with studies like that of Lott and Mustard is that they get the wrong answer on the linkage between firearms and crime, a larger problem is that they ask the wrong question. The distinctive problem in the United States is not rates of crime, but rather high rates of lethal violence.

The fruits of a new agenda

State legislation concerning handgun permits became an important issue for gun-owning groups only in the 1980s, and the reason for that prominence was a change in political tactics by the NRA. Prior to the 1980s, the lobbying efforts of the NRA and other gun owner interest groups were concentrated on the legislative branch of the federal government. By 1986 the gun lobby had succeeded in cutting back some coverage of the federal Gun Control Act of 1968, and the only important remaining legislative priority at the national level was opposition to a proposed handgun waiting period and police notification scheme that eventually passed Congress in 1993 as the Brady Bill.

This was the background for a decision by the NRA to invest more effort into increasing its influence at other levels of government. And for reasons of regional culture and the relative power of rural interests, the NRA had much more influence at the state level, particularly in the South, the West, and in rural regions. But the significant power of the gun lobby group in southern, western, and rural states was in one sense an embarrassment of riches. The very locations where the NRA possessed the most legislative influence had few restrictions on guns. It was necessary to provide a legislative agenda to match the political power that the gun groups had discovered.

The evident theory of requiring special permits is that concealed handguns in public places are a public danger unless restricted in quantity and given only to highly trustworthy citizens.

"Permit-to-carry" legislation provided the gun interests with an attractive state-level issue. Even states with few restrictions on ownership and transfer frequently required special permits before citizens could carry concealed firearms on their person or in a motor vehicle. State law usually prohibited carrying concealed weapons without a license, and either required the citizen to show good cause to obtain a license, or delegated discretion to issue or deny such special licenses to the chief law enforcement officer of the applicant's home community. The evident theory of requiring special permits is that concealed handguns in public places are a public danger unless restricted in quantity and given only to highly trustworthy citizens.

A competing theory is that all persons legally qualified to own guns should be allowed to carry them if they so desire. Adherence to this theory would entail either the abolition of the need for special licenses, or the relaxation of the standards for these licenses. The strategy chosen by the gun owner groups was to keep the need for a permit but to change state laws so that such permits would have to be issued to any citizen not disqualified by a serious criminal record, youth, mental illness, or other specially designated factor.

The states that recently adopted "shall issue" laws already had few restrictions on firearms.

In current vernacular these laws are called "shall issue" statutes. The focus on passing this style of permit-to-carry law has been more than modestly successful, especially in the South and the West. In the decade between 1977 and 1986, Lott and Mustard tell us that only one state passed a "shall issue" law: Maine in 1985. Between 1987 and 1991, however, eight jurisdictions passed statewide "shall issue" statutes, five in the South (Florida, Virginia, Georgia, West Virginia, Mississippi) and three in the West (Idaho, Oregon, and Montana). One additional state, Pennsylvania, enacted a "shall issue" law but excluded the state's largest city from the change.

This cursory survey of the legislative history of permit-to-carry reforms produces three conclusions that are important to assessing the Lott and Mustard study and others like it. First, the boomlet in "shall issue" legislation was a byproduct of the shift in gun lobby emphasis from the federal to the state level of government. During the generation prior to the mid-1980s, when the NRA concentrated its attention on Congress, the legal regulation of carrying concealed firearms was a nonissue. What made permits to carry a particularly attractive target of opportunity was that restrictive legislation was on the books even in many states where the gun lobby was strong.

Second, the passage of "shall issue" laws seems to have been championed as a symbolic rather than as an instrumental step. The rhetoric for reform was as an expansion of citizen rights, what gun owner groups call "firearms freedoms." There were no numerical targets for expanding licenses to carry that were emphasized by most gun-owning groups, and the focus of effort was not on follow-through after the new legislation achieved passage, but rather on achieving the legislative change. If the passage of such legislation was seen as an end in itself, rather than as a means to other objectives, it might not be prudent to expect extensive changes in citizen behavior as a result of the legislation.

And third, the collection of states that passed "shall issue" laws was in no sense a cross section of the American federal system. The regional pattern that distinguishes "shall issue" states from other jurisdictions are the differences one would predict. All of the state-wide "shall issue" legislation of the recent past, except that of Maine, occurred in southern and western states. The industrial midwest is missing from the roster of "shall issue" reform states, as is every state in the urban northeast except one. That one, Pennsylvania, is really the exception that proves the rule. What is urban and northeastern about Pennsylvania, the city of Philadelphia, was excluded from the coverage of the new law, a compromise that speaks volumes about the distinctive political constituency of "shall issue" laws.

The other predictable bias in the self-selected group of "shall issue" states is that the states that recently adopted "shall issue" laws already had few restrictions on firearms. This is hardly a surprise, but the fact that the states that passed these new laws were already unsympathetic to firearms control may limit the amount of change in behavior that we can expect as a consequence of the new law. The sort of state that passed a "shall issue" law in the 1980s is apt to be the same kind of place where ordinary citizens carrying concealed firearms might not be regarded as a major problem even before the law changed.

The problem with the distinct regional and legislative patterns that characterize the "shall issue" states is that they frustrate our capacity to compare trends in "shall issue" states with trends in other states. Because the states that changed legislation are different in location and constitution from the states that did not, comparisons across legislative categories will always risk confusing demographic and regional influences with the behavioral impact of different legal regimes.

The logic and findings of Lott and Mustard

The basic data and methodology of the Lott and Mustard study are the same as those of the multivariate econometric studies that have frequently been used to analyze aggregate crime statistics in search of policies that reduce crime. The trend in homicide and various other crime categories, as measured at the county level, is compared before and after the "shall issue" law went into effect.

The study, for example, examines trends in Idaho before and after its 1990 passage of a "shall issue" law to see whether the new law had an effect in Idaho. In order to do this, crime trends in Idaho, and other "shall issue" states, are compared with trends in the rest of the nation. If Idaho has 8 percent fewer homicides after the law came into effect than it would have had if it had followed national trends, the logic of the analysis would be to nominate that 8 percent difference as attributable to the change in law.

[There is] no attempt to measure carrying of handguns by citizens, use by citizens in self-defense from crime, or offender behavior in relation to street crime.

But, of course, Idaho is not the same as New York, and there seem to be systematic differences between those states that changed their standards for concealed weapons and those that did not. These differences between states may influence trends over time, as when crack cocaine impacted on very large eastern cities in the mid-1980s with a substantial impact on homicide levels. Do we want to compare Idaho, West Virginia, and Mississippi trends to Washington, D.C., and New York City trends over time?

Lott and Mustard are, of course, aware of this problem. Their solution, a standard econometric technique, is to build a statistical model that will control for all the differences between Idaho and New York City that influence homicide and crime rates, other than the "shall issue" laws. If one can "specify" the major influences on homicide, rape, burglary, and auto theft in our model, then we can eliminate the influence of these factors on the different trends. Lott and Mustard build models that estimate the effect of demographic data, economic data, and criminal punishment on various offenses. These models are the ultimate in statistical home cooking in that they are created for this data set by these authors and only tested on the data that will be used in the evaluation of the right-to-carry impacts.

> *The new carrying privilege would . . . not affect home or business self-defense but should have most of its preventive impact on street crime and offenses occurring in other public places.*

A criminologist would have a number of problems with both the model used in this study and the method of its validation. For example, the model assumes that the same short list of factors had the same degree of influence in all the states throughout the period. In the 1980s and early 1990s crack cocaine markets produced a wild expansion in homicide in New York City and Washington, D.C. (but not presumably in any Idaho counties), yet there is no account paid to this factor in the model.

It is important to note that Lott and Mustard are by no means isolated in their rather casual approach to modeling the causes of crime in this fashion. The techniques and assumptions used in this study have parallels in several other economic analyses of crime and punishment and in econometric analyses of other phenomena as well. Perhaps these methods are less problematic when used to explain forms of social and economic behavior besides crime. Perhaps not. But many of the methodological objections to this study can be made as well to a cluster of econometric examinations of crime and punishment.

Two idiosyncratic aspects of the Lott and Mustard analysis deserve special mention, however, and have an important influence on the power of these statistics as social science data about right-to-carry laws. In the first place, there is very little in the way of explicit theory advanced to explain where and when right-to-carry laws should operate as deterrents to the types of crime that can be frustrated by citizens carrying concealed handguns. The sort of fancy economic specification of behavioral impact that one usually finds in econometric contributions to legal studies is not present in this study. Indeed there is some ambiguity about the nature of the deterrent mechanism that is supposed to alter offenders' behavior. Figure 1 contrasts two different models of right-to-carry impact that would be consistent with effects found in the literature on deterrence.

The figure contrasts what we call the "Announcement" and "Crime Hazard" models of right-to-carry impact on crime. The announcement model expects that passing the new law, of and by itself, increases the anxiety of potential criminals and thus alters their behavior. This sort of

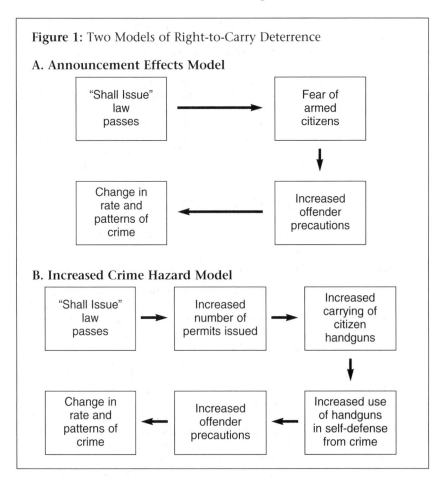

Figure 1: Two Models of Right-to-Carry Deterrence

A. Announcement Effects Model

B. Increased Crime Hazard Model

announcement effect was found by H. Lawrence Ross in his study of the impact of law enforcement crackdowns on drunk driving in Britain. Such effects are more likely when the change advertised is under the immediate and direct control of state authorities, and such effects tend to diminish over time.

It is more likely, however, that Lott and Mustard would adopt the crime hazard model, as it is more consistent with the rational choice and price metaphor approaches that economists tend to use when looking at crime. In this model, changes in law produce changes in the behavior of potential crime victims, which in turn alter the hazard associated with particular forms of crime and therefore lead to change in patterns and rates of crime.

An important failing

But this leads to the second important failing in Lott and Mustard that is not a recurrent feature in econometric studies. If it is a crime hazard model that Lott and Mustard are testing, they have no data to measure the critical intermediate steps between passing the legislation and reductions in crime rates. How can we know, for example, if the crime hazard model is correct when only the first and last steps (on which the two models are the same) are examined? After confirming that a "shall issue" statute was passed, Lott and Mustard make no attempt to measure carrying of handguns by citizens, use by citizens in self-defense from crime, or offender behavior in relation to street crime. There is merely the legislation and the crime data, linked only by the argument that no plausible rival hypothesis exists other than "shall issue" laws to explain the lower than predicted levels of selected crimes.

Inadequately detailed data is also a problem when comparing different types of crime. The political factors discussed earlier in this essay tell us that the legal change Lott and Mustard examine should only have impact on some types of crime. Handguns were freely available for home and business use in all the "shall issue" jurisdictions prior to the new laws. The new carrying privilege would thus not affect home or business self-defense but should have most of its preventive impact on street crime and offenses occurring in other public places. But the study contains no qualitative analysis of different patterns within crime categories to corroborate the right-to-carry prevention hypothesis. The connection is only between legislative activity in the first box of the two models in Figure 1 and aggregate crime categories in the last box.

So the evidence of causal linkage is quite fragile. If the model of crime is not good enough to control for the obvious differences between "shall issue" and other states, or if lower-than-expected violence levels are not consistently associated with the "shall issue" changes, or if the kinds of behavioral changes assumed by the deterrence model turn out not to take place, or if the kind of crime that is lower than expected is not of the type that can be plausibly tied to the carrying of concealed weapons—the causal attribution of the crime trends to the legal change is undone. Any single problem of significance in the list outlined above should invalidate the causal argument. What then should be the effect of finding significant problems under all four headings? We return to this issue at the end of the next section.

Deconstructing deterrence

In an age of the Internet and the computer, a good deal of reanalysis and reaction to a study can be launched prior to its actual scholarly publication. Because Lott and Mustard have cooperated by providing the data they analyzed to others, reanalysis of the data set emerged as a minor cottage industry in the autumn of 1996. We have examined three papers reporting on such statistical adventures, probably no more than a sample of the reanalysis that will take place in the near future. But this first work of reanalysis shows the vulnerability of the findings in many respects.

Dan Black and Daniel Nagin have produced one brief but wide-ranging reworking of Lott and Mustard's data under the auspices of the National Consortium on Violence Research. Their paper shows that the great bulk of the estimated prevention of homicide in Lott and Mustard is an artifact of excluding about 20,000 counties from the analysis of homicide because no offense-to-arrest ratio can be determined for those counties. Include those counties and the significant negative effect of right-to-carry on murder disappears. Black and Nagin also conclude that negative trends for robbery and aggravated assault that are estimated with the Lott and Mustard subsample of counties "vanish with the inclusion of the missing data." Murder, robbery, and aggravated assault had accounted for more than $6.1 billion of the savings the authors had claimed, about 95 percent of the net total. Easy come, easy go.

The deterrent effect of "shall carry" laws should be age specific because only adults are eligible to get permits, even in "shall issue" states.

Black and Nagin also use a different procedure to examine crime trends before and after the "shall issue" states passed those laws. Whereas Lott and Mustard found great consistency in the trends, Black and Nagin found that only Florida had marked changes after the laws were passed. The trends in the rest of the sample for most offenses look the same for two and three years after the new laws are passed as for two or three years before.

And when looking at specific crimes at the state level, Black and Nagin report no consistent statewide pattern of decline among the right-to-carry states. Instead, "Why do murders decline in Florida but increase in Virginia? Why do assaults fall in Maine but increase in Montana? In our view, the simultaneous existence of these significant positive and significant negative effects within the same crime category leads us to question the underlying econometric model used."

Black and Nagin are not alone in questioning the model used to explain crime and homicide. Both Albert Alschuler and Jens Ludwig note a number of problems in their separate papers. Why, for example, should the concentration of older black women in a population predict higher crime rates in the Lott and Mustard model, but not the increased concentration of young men, age 20 to 29, who are vastly more likely to commit such offenses?

Or consider the case of domestic killings. Of all the major subclasses of homicide, domestic killings are the least likely to involve streets and other public settings where a permit-to-carry law would make a difference in arming a victim. So this class of killings should not change if a new right-to-carry law is the reason homicide rates decline. Yet Alschuler points out that domestic homicide does decline more pronouncedly than acquaintance killing in the "shall issue" states. How can this be a result of a change in permit-to-carry policy?

Ludwig points out that the deterrent effect of "shall carry" laws should be age specific because only adults are eligible to get permits, even in "shall issue" states. This "adults only" phenomenon should have one of two different effects, depending on how seriously one takes a hazard model of criminal homicide causation. Either the killing of young victims should not be affected at all by the new laws, or it should actually increase as prospective killers seek out targets less threatening than the newly armed adults. In either case, the homicide rate for those older than 21 should decrease much more markedly than for the young victims who function as something of a control group because the permit-to-carry law did not change for them.

But this is not what happened in the seven "shall issue" states with a legal threshold of 21 in their laws. Further, in Pennsylvania, where a natural experiment was put in place by the state legislature, the proportion of young victims did not increase (as it should have) in those parts of the state under the new regime when compared over time with trends in Philadelphia (with no legal change). In fact, the young victim control group does slightly better than the adults for whom the policy changed. How could this possibly be the work of "shall issue" laws?

This kind of qualitative analysis produces a rather straightforward debunking of Lott and Mustard's central claim. But the arbitrariness and superficiality of their study do not set it apart from many other regression studies of crime and punishment. Just as Messrs. Lott and Mustard can, with one model of the determinants of homicide, produce statistical residuals suggesting that "shall issue" laws reduce homicide, we expect that a determined econometrician can produce a treatment of the same historical periods with different models and opposite effects. Econometric modeling is a double-edged sword in its capacity to facilitate statistical findings to warm the hearts of true believers of any stripe. But the same overwhelming problems will haunt studies that point the multivariate arrow in a different direction. It is not just that these authors did research in the wrong way, they did the wrong sort of research.

A note on justifiable homicide

None of the first round of critiques of Lott and Mustard dealt with the absence of any measurement of citizen self-defense, so we collected some of our own data on the topic. Recall that the subject of the Lott and Mustard study is the effect of citizens carrying handguns on the rate of homicide and other crimes. Yet there are no measures, direct or indirect, of civilian handgun carrying in any state, at any time covered by the study. The authors just assume a positive impact of "shall carry" laws on handgun carrying behavior.

One imperfect measure of armed citizens' defense against crime in the street can be found in the Supplemental Homicide Reports prepared by police departments and collected by the Federal Bureau of Investigation. Killings regarded as justified by the police are separately counted for police and for civilians. The number of justified killings by civilians over time is available as a measure of trends in armed self-defense. Using a body count of justifiable civilian killings as a measure of the use of concealed firearms that prevented crime is both an undercount and overcount in important respects. But the trend in killings over time might still be a useful indicator of the trend in self-defense episodes over time.

As this was written, we had access to a CD-ROM that provided homicide data from the Supplementary Homicide Reports for the years 1976 through 1991. We examined whether the six states that passed "shall issue" laws prior to 1990 had experienced changes in justifiable killings inflicted by civilians when the two calendar years prior to the year when the law was passed were compared to the two calendar years after the law was enacted.

The pattern that emerges from this sounding is anything but uniform. Acceptable data on homicide of any kind are not available for the state of Florida. Virginia and Georgia report more justifiable killings in the two years after passage than in the two years before. Maine and West Virginia have low levels of justifiable killing throughout the time series and fewer justifiable killings in the two years after the year of passage than in the two years before. Maine, in fact, had no justifiable homicides in the six years following the implementation of the law. In Pennsylvania, justifiable killings outside of Philadelphia went down, while justifiable killings in the city increased—the reverse of the trend one would predict on the basis of the legislation.

Bottom lines

Some day there will be a good evaluation of "shall issue" legislation on the behavior and the welfare of citizens. It will focus on the experience of one or two jurisdictions, not ten at a time. It will collect detailed data on the people who take out permits and how such permits influence their behavior in situations when they feel threatened while they are carrying guns. The study will probably find some modest costs associated with laws that appear to result in fewer than 2 percent of citizens taking out these permits, and might find some modest benefits as well. Large reductions in violence are quite unlikely because they would be out of proportion to the small scale of the change in carrying firearms that the legislation produced.

The Lott and Mustard study will not help to build a bridge to this kind of detailed knowledge of the effect of "shall carry" laws. The regression study they report is an all-or-nothing proposition as far as knowledge of legal impact is concerned. If the model is wrong, if their bottom line estimates of impact cannot withstand scrutiny, there is no intermediate knowledge of the laws' effects on behavior that can help us sort out the manifold effects of such legislation. As soon as we find flaws in the major conclusions, the regression analyses tell us nothing. What we know from this study about the effects of "shall carry" laws is, therefore, nothing at all. Nevertheless, let the buyer beware. This study has already entered the policy debate and will no doubt be fuel for "shall issue" proponents in all the states that have not yet enacted such legislation.

Any policy that accepts the present handgun inventory in the United States as immutable will be responsible for continuing high rates of lethal violence in the foreseeable American future.

It is by no means impossible that some crime is prevented by increased citizen gun carrying in some U.S. states. How much crime and under what circumstances are empirical questions. But one other important fact makes the policy impact of such laws less important. The benefits and costs of permits to carry are marginal to the tremendous costs we already pay for the high ownership and use of handguns in the United States. What sets the United States apart from other developed countries is not our high crime rates. What sets the United States apart is our distinctively high rates of lethal violence. Our cities have no more property crime than major cities abroad. Even the rates of assault reported in other industrial nations are quite close to the assault rate in the United States. But the rate of violent death from assault in the United States is from 4 to 18 times as high as in other G7 nations; and this is largely a consequence of the widespread use of handguns in assaults and robberies. Firearms are only involved in about 4 percent of all American crime, but are used in 70 percent of all fatal assaults.

Laws that encourage the licensing of citizens to carry concealed handguns are similar in one respect to waiting periods for handgun purchase and federal legislation intended to produce "gun free" elementary and secondary schools. They are attempts to fine-tune citizen behavior in an atmosphere dominated by the free availability and widespread use of guns in violence. For those who hope for the substantial reduction in lethal violence in the United States, this effort at fine-tuning seems very much like rearranging the deck chairs on the Titanic. Any policy that accepts the present handgun inventory in the United States as immutable will be responsible for continuing high rates of lethal violence in the foreseeable American future.

7

Banning Handguns Would Reduce Crime

Robert F. Drinan

Robert F. Drinan is a Jesuit priest and a professor at Georgetown University Law Center.

Countries that have rigid controls on gun ownership, such as Canada, experience low homicide rates compared to the United States, where guns are more readily available. The United States could match other countries' homicide rates if gun possession was outlawed or severely restricted.

In the outpouring of grief and incomprehension surrounding the schoolyard shooting in Jonesboro, Arkansas, in which four students and one teacher died [in March 1998], most observers probably failed to note that the 13-year-old boy who killed one of his classmates had just completed a course in marksmanship; he learned well because, just as directed, he shot his victim directly through the heart.

America's gun culture

The gun culture is deep in America. It traces its origins to the Wild West and the age of instant retaliation against Indians and anyone who impeded a rugged individualist. But, one has to ask again and again, can this explain a nation with over 60 million handguns and the highest homicide rate of any nation on the earth?

The nation is weary of this tired and tedious question. But the appalling repetition of the slaughter of the innocents compels us to focus on guns.

Some years ago, an institute at Harvard University had a program comparing the way in which Canada and the United States treat guns. The contrast is striking. Canada has rigid controls on the possession and sale of guns, and their homicide rate is one of the lowest in the world. Canada follows the tradition of Mother England. There the strict regula-

Reprinted from Robert F. Drinan, "For Our Kids' Sake, Let's End the Fatal Attraction to Guns," *National Catholic Reporter*, August 14, 1998, with permission.

tion of guns was made even more stringent in 1996 when, after a school massacre in Dunblane, England banned all handguns.

The experts at the Harvard conference pointed to the fact that Congress has defied the recommendations of five presidential commissions, all of which urged the strictest controls on guns. It was also noted that the Reagan and Bush administrations yielded to the 3 million-member National Rifle Association. But in the end, the panel at Harvard had to admit that there is some unexplainable obsession in the American psyche that needs guns.

For Americans it is embarrassing not to be able to explain, much less reverse, a mania that results in international shame. In 1996, handguns killed 15 in Japan, 30 in Britain, 211 in Germany and 9,390 in the United States! In 1997, the firearms-related death rate among American children under 15 was nearly six times higher than that of children in all 25 other industrial nations combined.

Guns should be severely curbed for adults and forbidden for children.

The United States never seems to be ready for gun control. When President Reagan was shot and wounded, the hope was that the country would be ready for reform. But even the attempted murder of the pope about the same time did not impel the Congress to act.

It is overwhelmingly clear that America wants to keep its guns. Since 1985, 31 states have passed laws that allow persons not only to carry guns but to conceal them. Some gun lovers even claim that the increase in the number of concealed guns has reduced the crime rate!

The market for guns is so saturated that the gun manufacturers have now turned their attention to the youth market. This is one more reason for the slaughter of school children.

The entire law enforcement community continues to lobby for more gun control ordinances like the Brady Bill. Police organizations reject the erroneous and spurious interpretation of the Second Amendment proclaimed by the National Rifle Association. But even the police cannot persuade the Congress or state legislatures to outlaw the possession of guns among those under the age of 18 or 21.

Is there some way by which the media could have prevented the lonely and disturbed boys in Jonesboro, Arkansas, and Springfield, Oregon, from acting out their obsessions? Is there a streak of violence in the American character? For 40 years the United States threatened the Soviet empire with extinction by nuclear weapons. The nation is prepared to execute 3,300 inmates on death row. The people of America allow 1.6 million abortions each year.

How to reduce the homicide rate

With sustained efforts the United States could reduce its homicide rate by guns to the equivalent of Canada where 106 persons were killed by guns in 1997.

It seems almost inevitable that more massacres of children will occur. There will always be some disturbed youths among the 47 million school children in the country. But at least the access of these persons to guns can be eliminated. Toleration of guns in America is an anachronism. Guns should be severely curbed for adults and forbidden for children.

The Catholic bishops of America said it well in 1978: "We believe that handguns should be effectively controlled and eventually eliminated from our society."

8

Banning Handguns
Does Not Reduce Crime

Don B. Kates

*Don B. Kates is a criminologist, lawyer, and professor. He is the author
of* Guns and Violence *and co-editor of* The Great American Gun Debate. *He wishes to acknowledge the contribution of Mr. C.B. Kates to
the following article.*

Many European countries have stricter gun control laws than the
United States, yet their suicide and homicide rates are higher than
America's. It is pointless to argue that banning guns would reduce
crime. A country's violence rate is not determined by the availability of guns but by the society's cultural, social, economic, and
institutional values.

Americans have been gravely misled about foreign gun ownership and
the severity and effectiveness of foreign gun bans. It simply is not
true to state that "the U.S. has more gun availability and far less restric-
tion than any other modern industrial nation."

That honor goes to Israel where, nevertheless, murder "rates are
much lower than in the United States despite . . . [Israel's] greater availability of guns to law-abiding civilians," writes Israeli judge Abraham Ten-
nenbaum (formerly an official with the Israeli National Police and then a
professor of criminology).

Israel

Israeli law requires that a person have a license in order to own any kind
of firearm, but the license is readily available to any law-abiding adult
who can show he or she has had firearms training. (Israel has universal
military training for Jews of both sexes.) And if you legally possess a gun,
Israel allows—indeed encourages—carrying it. In effect, Israeli law nearly
parallels that of Florida, Pennsylvania and 28 other U.S. states where licenses to carry a concealed firearm are available on application and passing a background check. (Vermonters have the right to carry without obtaining a license.)

Reprinted from Don B. Kates, "Gun Laws Around the World: Do They Work?" *American Guardian*,
October 1997, with permission.

Nevertheless, though rapidly growing, gun *ownership* is low in Israel—because it is unnecessary. Israel is a socialist country, so the government is supposed to provide people all their basic needs, including guns for self-defense. Israel loans out guns by the millions to its citizens.

Israelis going to a dangerous area routinely stop by a police station or communal armory to pick up an Uzi or a pistol. Israeli policy is that armed guardians should be near every place there are potential victims. Schools may not send children on field trips unless the children are accompanied by at least one teacher or parent carrying a gun.

At night, many neighborhoods are patrolled by "civil guards"—teenage volunteers carrying government-issued guns. If someone has disappeared (and possibly has been kidnapped), dozens, scores or even hundreds of civilian volunteer searchers are assembled and issued firearms to carry while searching for the missing person.

So widespread is this issuing of arms that it fundamentally affects Israeli firearms training. Since most pistols are not personally owned,

---

Table 1: International Suicide/Homicide Table*

(*Ranked according to highest combined
suicide-murder rate; nations ranked higher than the
U.S. in either suicide or murder rates are in bold face)

COUNTRY	YEAR	SUICIDE	MURDER	COMBINED
Estonia	1995	**39.99**	**22.11**	62.1
Russia	1992	**26.6**	**15.3**	41.9
Latvia	1990	**26.**	9.2	35.2
Lithuania	1990	**26.**	7.5	33.5
Finland	1994–95	**27.3**	3.3	30.6
Ukraine	1990	**20.6**	8.0	28.6
Denmark	1991	**22.**	5.0	27.0
Austria	1991	**22.3**	1.5	23.8
Switzerland*	1994–95	**20.8**	1.1	21.9
France	1990	**20.2**	1.1	21.3
Belgium	1987	**19.3**	1.4	20.7
United States*	1995–96	11.5	7.3	18.8
Sweden	1990	**17.2**	1.3	18.5
Germany	1995	**15.8**	1.8	17.6
Luxembourg	1991	**15.1**	2.1	17.2
New Zealand	1989	**13.9**	1.9	15.8
Canada	1995	**12.9**	2.0	14.9
Israel	1989	7.3	1.2	8.5

*All information in this table dated before 1993 comes from the *U.N. Demographic Yearbooks* for 1993 and 1992. All information dated 1993 and thereafter comes from a draft study prepared for the U.N. Commission on Crime Prevention and Criminal Justice's Vienna Session 28 April–9 May, 1997, *except:* a) the U.S. homicide figure comes from FBI preliminary data for 1996, and b) the Swiss homicide and suicide rates come from the Swiss national police.

Israelis are trained to keep them in "Condition 2" (cartridges in magazine, but not chambered). This is because the pistol a trainee may be issued at any particular future time could be any of the myriad of guns in Israeli arsenals: A Browning M-35 (Hi-Power); a Walther P-38; a Beretta Modello 1951 (Brigadeer); or even a French Modeles 1935A or 1950, or the Polish Pistolet wz/35 (Radom) or Czech CZ vz/27.

Americans have been gravely misled about foreign gun ownership and the severity and effectiveness of foreign gun bans.

No matter how unfamiliar the recipient may be with a pistol issued him, one technique suits all: Condition 2 is a safe method of carry when there is no need for immediate use, and when all one need do is jack the slide to have the firearm ready for use.

Israel's "guns everywhere" policy accounts for incidents such as the one in which three terrorists opened up with AK-47s on a Jerusalem crowd. The terrorists were able to kill only one victim before they were themselves shot down by handgun-carrying Israelis.

The surviving terrorist was bitter when he spoke to the press the next day. Their plan had been to quickly kill 20 or 30 people at a series of public places, always escaping before military or police could arrive. They hadn't known Israeli civilians were armed. The terrorist felt that it just wasn't "fair."

Incidentally, this occurred with three weeks of the massacre of 21 unarmed victims in a San Ysidro, California, McDonald's fast-food restaurant.

Europe

Equally erroneous is the impression that Europe is uniformly anti-gun. Laws vary. Luxembourg totally bans all guns from civilian ownership. France, Belgium and Germany allow citizens to own handguns but these countries are more restrictive than most U.S. states. In Austria, every law-abiding citizen has a legal right to buy handguns, and roughly ten per cent of Austrians have done so (compared to 16 per cent of U.S. citizens).

Switzerland

And then there is Switzerland, where the laws are similar to those in Israel and gun availability is comparable to that in the U.S. In Switzerland, handgun licenses are available to any law-abiding applicant. In half the Swiss cantons (similar to U.S. states), licensees are free to carry their personal handguns concealed. Beyond this freedom of ownership, every law-abiding military-age Swiss male is issued a firearm and he must keep it at home to perform his mandatory militia obligation.

For the 263,000 officers and noncommissioned officers, the issued firearm is a 9 mm Parabellum semi-automatic pistol, either the SIG-Sauer P210 or its successor, the SIG-Sauer P220. For the millions of enlisted men, the issued firearm is an assault rifle: the STGW 90. The STGW 90 is a version of the SIG-Sauer 550 semi-automatic rifle that is select-fire, meaning it may be fired in either full- or semi-auto mode. When he retires, any Swiss militiaman who wishes to buy his issued firearm may do so.

Homicides in Europe

Homicide rates are quite low in all the nations mentioned above. However, the homicide rate in handgun-banning Luxembourg is much higher than in the others: 2.1 per 100,000 population, versus 1.2 and 1.1 per 100,000 for "handgun-ridden" Israel and Switzerland—which have the lowest homicide rates of all. (The accompanying table provides the references for homicide and suicide rate comparisons discussed in this article.)

Western Europe, in fact, has always had very low homicide rates as compared to the U.S. This is not something caused by strict anti-gun laws, because this low homicide rate existed before such laws were adopted, and the low rate occurs also in Switzerland and Austria which have no such strict anti-gun laws.

Whatever their purpose, European anti-gun laws have miserably failed.

European anti-gun laws only arrived after World War I, and they were not passed in order to curb crime. They were passed in response to the political violence of that tumultuous era (1918–1939) between the two World Wars.

Whatever their purpose, European anti-gun laws have miserably failed. They have not prevented assassination, terrorism, and other political violence—problems occurring throughout Europe on a fairly regular basis, but not so in the U.S. Neither have these anti-gun laws stopped non-political crime, which has steadily increased throughout Europe since World War II.

To this issue, the further question has been asked, "Why has Europe had so much less non-political violent crime than the U.S.? Yale University's preeminent historian, Dr. C. Vann Woodward, suggests an answer. He writes, "The impact upon Europe of the emigration [to the U.S.] of 35,000,000 Europeans in the Century between the Napoleonic Wars and World War I remains to be acknowledged. The importance of the West as a safety valve for American society has undoubtedly been exaggerated. But the significance of America as a safety valve for Europe and the effect of the closing of that safely valve after World War I remain to be fully assessed."[1]

Suicides in Europe

Nor, finally, have these anti-gun laws stopped suicide, something which has always been a much greater problem in Europe than in the U.S. In this respect, one can note a curious (but invariable) omission when anti-gun articles compare the U.S. to Europe.[2]

Anti-gun propaganda emphasizes suicide as well as homicide. U.S. suicide rates have risen over the past quarter century (while U.S. homicide rates have declined). However, anti-gun advocates recently have taken to combining suicide and homicide figures in the U.S. This allows them to conceal the decline in U.S. homicide rates (and to exaggerate the so-called "societal costs" of gun ownership). They have done this more particularly in the last few years while the U.S. homicide rate has been declining (despite a 100 per cent increase in handgun ownership since the 1970s).

But then, inconsistently, when comparing the U.S. to Europe, they only compare the homicide rates. They never use the combined homicide-suicide figure—because it would refute their entire argument; it shows that Europe's homicide-suicide combined rates are higher than that of the U.S.

Combined homicide-suicide

Look to the accompanying table for the result obtained when the anti-gun forces' combined homicide-suicide approach is applied to the international figures: The U.S. combined homicide-suicide rate falls in the middle of the nations, and is lower than [eleven] nations. Even compared to the nations with lower combined rates, the U.S. rate is only slightly higher.

Of the 18 nations shown in the table, the U.S. ranks in the middle as to murder and suicide combined. The lowest rate of all is for Israel, the nation where guns are the most available and supplied to citizens, including teenagers.

My point is not that gun availability reduces suicide, or even murder. Statistics show that the relatively crime-free nations don't appear to need or benefit from severe anti-gun laws.

Western Europe

The table clearly shows that, regardless of their gun laws, Western European nations have roughly comparable rates of both murder and suicide. This cannot plausibly be attributed to severe handgun restrictions because the highest murder rates among these nations are in the nations with the most restrictive gun laws (Luxembourg, Denmark, Germany). In those restrictive nations, the average murder rate of 2.73 per 100,000 population is over twice as high as the 1.26 average rate of Switzerland, Israel and Austria, where gun laws are least restrictive.

Russia and the Baltic countries

Even less do gun control laws benefit high crime nations like Russia and its former possessions, the countries of Estonia, Latvia, Lithuania and the Ukraine. When these and other countries were under the control of the former Union of Soviet Socialist Republics, the central Soviet government totally banned civilian handgun ownership.

The Soviet government uniquely implemented the ban by creating after World War II a unique caliber cartridge for Soviet handguns (9 × 18 mm). This cartridge is too short to interchange with handguns using the familiar European standard 9 × 19 cartridge (9 mm Parabellum, or 9 mm Luger, as Americans commonly call it); it's too long to interchange with handguns shooting the .380 cartridge. This meant that anyone smuggling foreign handguns into the USSR (for example, soldiers returning from foreign wars) would find ammunition unavailable.[3] Nevertheless, though exact statistics were never released, analysis clearly indicates that Soviet homicide rates far exceeded those in the U.S.[4]

The highest murder rates among these nations are in the nations with the most restrictive gun laws.

With the USSR no longer in existence, the homicide rates in the former Soviet republics and Russia continue to exceed those in the U.S., as shown in the accompanying table. Under the Soviet regime, with strict gun control, the weapons used for homicides were largely knives, clubs, and other non-firearms. Today, though handguns remain virtually unavailable to ordinary Russian citizens, homicide rates remain high, being committed by those criminals in Russia, Latvia, Lithuania, etc., who seem to have no difficulty acquiring both Russian and foreign-made handguns and suitable ammunition.

Violence in any society

Such international statistics show the pointlessness of gun bans. In any society, truly violent people are only a small minority. We know that law-abiding citizens do not commit violent crimes. We also know that criminals will neither obey gun bans nor refrain rom turning other deadly instruments to their nefarious purposes.

It is obvious and well-proven that the amount of violence in any particular society is determined not by the mere availability of any particular form of weapon, but by cultural, socioeconomic and institutional factors that produce people willing to engage in extreme violence.[5]

How much violence occurs in any given society will depend on the proportionate size of truly violent people.

In sum, peaceful societies do not need general gun bans and violent societies do not benefit from them.

Notes

1. C. Van Woodward, *The Future of the Past* (Oxford University Press 1989), pp. 93–94.

2. Don B. Kates, Henry E. Schaffer, et al., "Guns and Public Health: Epidemic of Violence or Pandemic of Propaganda," 62 *Tennessee Law Review* 513, 561–65 (1995).

3. Randy E. Barnett & Don B. Kates, "Under fire: The New consensus on the Second Amendment," 45 *Emory Law Journal* 1139, 1238–39 (1996).

4. See David Shipler, *Russia: Broken Idols, Solemn Dreams* (New York Times Books, 1983), pp. 129 and 231.

5. Don B. Kates and Gary Kleck, *The Great American Gun Debate: Essays in Firearms and Violence* (Pacific Research Institute 1997), Introduction, Ch. 1.

9

Banning Assault-Type Rifles Would Reduce Crime

Dianne Feinstein

Dianne Feinstein is a U.S. senator from California.

The ban on the manufacture and sale of assault weapons has been effective at reducing gun violence. As the availability of the assault weapons is restricted, the number of people who have been killed or injured by assault weapons has declined, as well as the number of semiautomatic rifles used in crimes. The American public is very supportive of the assault weapons ban despite the efforts of the pro-gun lobby to repeal it. The assault weapons ban should not be repealed.

Common sense tells one that no hunter or recreational sportsman should need a military-style assault weapon to shoot a deer, duck or clay pigeon. If they do, they might consider taking up bowling instead.

But after a hard-won ban on the manufacture and sale of these weapons was passed by Congress in 1994, the National Rifle Association, or NRA, and their stalwart supporters in the House and Senate want to repeal this legislation [the ban has not been repealed]. The ban prohibits 19 types of semiautomatic weapons with high-capacity magazines. The NRA calls it "cosmetic" and repeatedly has said that it is not working.

Why, then, is the NRA working so feverishly to repeal it? The reason is that even though the ban has been in effect for only 14 months, there are signs it is, in fact, having an impact.

Assault weapons statistics

Nationally, there has been a decrease in the use of assault weapons in crimes. The best information about the types of guns used in crimes can be found in police requests to the Bureau of Alcohol, Tobacco and Firearms, or ATF, to trace the sources of guns and where and when such weapons have been purchased. In 1993, the year before the ban went into effect, the 19 assault weapons banned by name under current law accounted for 8.2 percent of all ATF gun traces. The ban became effective on Sept. 13, 1994; from that date through November 1995, assault weapons composed only 4.3 percent of all gun traces—nearly a 50 percent decrease.

The use of such weapons to kill police officers also has declined. In 1994, when the ban was not in effect for most of the year, a study by Handgun Control Inc. found that assault weapons and guns with high-capacity magazines accounted for 41 percent of police gun deaths where the make and model of the weapon were known. In 1995, the figure fell to 28.6—a 30 percent decrease.

Supply and demand

Perhaps most important is the impact of the ban on the availability of such weapons. Because the supply is decreasing, prices are going up. A survey conducted by my office yielded the following information for three of the most widely used assault weapons:

• A December 1993 issue of *Shotgun News* listed an SKS Paratrooper assault rifle for $99.95. The advertisement added, "This may be your last chance to buy at these prices!" The same weapon was offered in the November 1995 issue of the magazine for $129—a 30 percent increase—with the word *banned* in bold letters.

• *Shotgun News* offered the Norinco AK-47 for $695 in December 1993. By December 1995, the price had gone up to $850 and, according to the friendly clerk on the phone, only one remained for sale.

• In 1993, *Shotgun News* listed new Uzis for $795. By December 1995, the price was $995—a 25 percent increase.

Supplies are down. Prices are up. And they will continue to go up as these weapons become more and more difficult to find. The ban is working.

The attempt to repeal

Yet despite these very real gains in making assault weapons more difficult to obtain; despite the decline in the use of assault weapons against police officers and in all crimes; and despite sound reasoning and the will of 72 percent of the American people according to recent polls, opponents of the ban are determined to reverse course and repeal it.

Common sense tells one that no hunter or recreational sportsman should need a military-style assault weapon to shoot a deer, duck or clay pigeon.

Their relentless zeal is dumbfounding. Who besides drug dealers, gang members and revenge killers needs these weapons of war? Who do the politicians who are so willing to follow the NRA off a cliff like lemmings think they represent? Certainly not the public, who want these guns off the streets. Certainly not law-enforcement officers, who risk their lives against these weapons every day and strongly support the ban. A report released in January 1996 by the Center for Public Integrity provides a clue. Take Sen. Phil Gramm of Texas—a vocal opponent of the assault-weapons ban and a candidate for the 1996 Republican presidential nomination. The center's report, which tracked campaign contributions to various candidates, showed that the NRA is Gramm's biggest "lifetime patron," giving more than $440,000 to his political campaigns. The report also indicates that Gramm has not disappointed his benefactors, supporting the organization's interests on 18 major gun bills.

Last year [1995] I received a letter from a constituent, Carole Ann Taylor of Los Angeles, whose 17-year-old son, Willie, was, killed by a shot in the back from an assault weapon. "After 17 years of loving, nurturing and guiding my only child, Willie, through birthday parties, Boy Scouts, basketball games, job interviews, Christmases and many other joy-filled events," she wrote, "someone with an accomplice—an AK-47—ended my son's life on a residential street as my son stood talking with a girlfriend on the sidewalk."

"I ask the 104th Congress," she continued, "was I in error to raise my son to live in a civilized society, or would military training for war have been more appropriate in sustaining his life? If, in fact, this is a civilized society, the assault weapon must remain on the ban list."

I couldn't agree more.

10

Banning Assault-Type Rifles Would Not Reduce Crime

Joseph Perkins

Joseph Perkins is an editorial writer for the San Diego Union-Tribune.

The semiautomatic weapons prohibited under the assault weapons ban are no different than other semiautomatic guns which are legal. All semiautomatic weapons fire only one bullet per trigger pull and are no more powerful or deadly than other guns. Furthermore, these weapons are rarely used in the commission of a crime. Banning these weapons will not reduce crime rates. The ban is simply part of an attempt to ban all semiautomatic weapons.

Hardly any American would dispute that there is far too much gun-related violence in our society. Not when there are more gun deaths in the United States each year than in any other nation in the civilized world.

The politicians would have the crime-fearing public believe that the simple way to reduce gun-related violence is to enact more gun controls. Thus, President Clinton's recent executive order banning importation of nearly six dozen types of so-called "assault weapons."

"As everyone knows, you don't need an Uzi to go deer hunting," the president said, with 15 uniformed law enforcement officers standing behind him in what the White House described as a silent show of support. "You don't need an AK-47 to go skeet shooting. These are military weapons of war."

Now one needn't be a "gun extremist"—the latest put-down assigned to folks who fear erosion of their Second Amendment right to keep and bear arms—to take issue with the president's remarks or to question the efficacy of his executive order.

Indeed, based on the president's sound bite, you would think that, until his executive order last week, the nation's gun sellers were importing Uzis and AK-47s like they were going out of style. But, in fact, these weapons were already banned under a provision of the 1994 crime bill.

The White House claims that the 58 semiautomatic weapons covered under the president's executive order are variations of the Uzi and AK-47.

Reprinted from Joseph Perkins, "Banning Semiautomatics Won't Stop Violence," *San Diego Union-Tribune*, April 17, 1998, with permission.

They accuse foreign gun makers of making cosmetic changes to get around the 1994 assault weapons ban.

But the White House is exploiting the public's ignorance of differences between semiautomatic and automatic weapons. The Israeli-made Uzi and Russian-made AK-47 are automatic rifles that fire multiple rounds with each pull of the trigger, much like a rapid-fire machine gun.

The semiautomatic "assault weapons" that the president banned fire only one round per trigger pull, which is quite different from the "weapons of war" that the president talked about.

Moreover, notes John Lott Jr., a fellow at the University of Chicago School of Law, the 58 imported "assault weapons" banned by the president are no different than semiautomatic weapons sold here in the United States.

"Assault weapons" . . . account for fewer than 1 percent of firearms recovered at crime scenes.

"They are not more powerful," according to Lott, "they don't shoot any faster and they don't shoot any more rounds. Indeed," he continues, "the particular guns that were banned use smaller cartridges—and thus possess less killing power—than standard hunting rifles."

And here's something else the crime-fearing public ought to know about so-called "assault weapons"—they account for fewer than 1 percent of firearms recovered at crime scenes. Indeed, more Americans are bludgeoned to death each year than are murdered by semiautomatic rifles.

But the president doesn't want to hear this—because it undermines the administration's effort to broaden the definition of "assault weapons" as part of its unspoken, incremental effort to ban semiautomatic rifles. The White House also doesn't want to acknowledge that, while many of the nation's police chiefs pay lip service to the administration's gun control agenda, rank and file cops feel differently.

This was borne out by a 1997 survey of 2,000 sworn members of the San Diego Police Department which revealed that 82 percent opposed an assault weapons ban, 94 percent said that recent gun laws (including weapons bans, magazine capacity limits and longer waiting periods) have not reduced violent crime in their service area, and 92 percent said that further restrictive gun laws will not decrease violent crime.

The sentiments of these San Diego police officers were perhaps best expressed by Officer Roy Huntington, in a commentary he authored last year. "Cops," he wrote, "are disgusted with being ordered to pose formally behind self-appointed 'community leaders' and governmental bigwigs for publicity photos. This serves to convey the illusion we support the uninformed garbage they are attempting to foist upon an often sadly unsuspecting public."

Indeed, it would be wondrous if the president's latest ban on imported semiautomatic rifles reduced the amount of gun-related violence in this country. But the president knows—and the American people ought to know—that it will have less than zero effect.

11

Law-Abiding Citizens Do Not Need Assault-Type Rifles

Lucian K. Truscott IV

Lucian K. Truscott IV is an author.

The gun culture in America has changed. Guns were once expensive to purchase and were used only for hunting. Now people shoot at targets designed to look like human figures and collect weapons whose only purpose is to kill people. The information and technology to transform semiautomatic guns into fully automatic and therefore, illegal, weapons are readily available from gun magazines and over the Internet. For a ban on assault weapons to be effective, people must be prosecuted and imprisoned for breaking America's gun laws.

Growing up as an Army brat in the 1950's and 60's, I could have been a poster boy for the National Rifle Association. When I was 12, I started competing in N.R.A.-sponsored shooting contests every Saturday morning. When I was 13, I was given my first single-shot 16-gauge shotgun as a Christmas present and started going hunting with my father and brother in the forests surrounding the Army posts and small rural towns where we lived.

At 18, I went to West Point and qualified as an expert marksman on the M-14 rifle, M-16 rifle and .45-caliber pistol. Later, in the Army, I taught classes in the safe use of those and many other weapons.

The gun culture

I've got no objections to owning guns. What bothers me is how the culture of guns has changed. When I was young, guns were expensive. Our neighbors owned only one or two guns, and they were only used for hunting. Now many gun owners collect assault rifles that have no practical use other than to kill people.

President Clinton announced that he plans to ban the import of 58 types of military assault weapons permanently. In his remarks he said foreign gun makers were making minor cosmetic modifications on guns to skirt the law, and that's what prompted his decision.

I support the ban, but it's questionable how much of an effect his action will have. A recent tour of gun-culture sites on the Internet and a perusal of 10 gun magazines revealed that the country is already flooded with legal sniper rifles and military-style submachine guns, along with the information and technology necessary to convert them to be fully automatic.

It's not abnormal today for individual gun owners to have 50 or more guns—the approximate number of weapons an entire infantry platoon would carry. These gun fanatics are not veterans or interested in joining the military or even a local paramilitary group. Instead, they prefer to play-act roles in a fantasy military and spend weekends at "practical shooting" courses, a term which entered the national lexicon when it was reported that one of the children charged in the Jonesboro killings attended such courses with his father.

It's insanity for military-style assault weapons to be cheaper and more easily obtainable than an American-made hunting rifle.

"Practical shooting" may not sound that different from going to a shooting range and hitting bull's-eye targets. But I've been to a "practical shooting" course in Louisiana, and it's far more disturbing. You walk through the shooting range as human-silhouette targets pop up. You fire at the silhouettes, knocking down and "killing" the targets as you go, an exercise eerily similar to one I went through in the Army. Practical? It's practical only as military training to kill human beings.

Now children wear camouflage outfits to school, and men in combat-style fatigues and boots walk around Wal-Mart looking as if they were just back from patrol in Bosnia. At a wedding I attended recently in a rural area of the South, I saw at least one young man wearing a camouflage shirt.

Sniper rifles

For reasons that escape me entirely, an entire subculture has developed around sniper rifles. A gun enthusiast of my acquaintance proudly constructed his own sniper rifle from a separate barrel, trigger assembly, bolt action and stock. He uses the word "sniper" in his E-mail address. A recent issue of *Guns & Ammo* magazine has a long feature on a sniper rifle, the Kel-Tec Sub-9 folding carbine, which informs readers that a test-firing of the Sub-9 produced a result "good enough for a head shot at 100 yards and quite good enough (if you get the bullet drop right) for a body shot at 150-plus yards."

Who steals your car or breaks into your house from 100 to 150 yards away? The only possible explanation for the celebration of high-powered sniper weapons and night scopes and camouflage fatigues is fantasy fulfillment for gun fanatics. This stuff isn't "practical," it's deadly.

Shooting rifles at bull's-eyes in competition can be loads of fun. Going hunting after rabbits with a shotgun can be challenging. Other weapons are useful for self-defense. I still own two guns: a small-caliber revolver my wife used to carry when we lived in a bad neighborhood in New Orleans, and a .357 Magnum revolver I picked up at a gun show for $85. I once carried it into a housing project to recover our stolen car.

But today guns don't need to have a purpose—they are a way of life in and of themselves. And the N.R.A. defends that idea every time it insists that people have a right to own an assault weapon.

When the N.R.A. spends millions of dollars to lobby against laws that stipulate mandatory gun-safety courses or that create a system to license guns the same way we license cars, it is encouraging an irresponsible gun culture that supplants responsible gun ownership.

When you get in the Army, you spend a week on weapons safety procedures and learn to assemble, disassemble and clean your weapon, often blindfolded and in a dark room. You carry your weapon everywhere. You eat with it by your side, and you sleep with it. Then, and only then, does a team of expert marksmen take you to a supervised firing range and teach you how to shoot it.

Compare the Army's training with laws in states like Arkansas, where it's legal for a 10-year-old to own a semiautomatic assault weapon without a moment of safety instruction, training in how to shoot it or adult supervision.

The N.R.A. is determined to preserve these "rights," and will no doubt challenge the President's proposed ban on many imported assault weapons, with the usual argument that it will lead to a ban on all guns. What the N.R.A. actually accomplishes is making sniper rifles, submachine guns and the $89 Russian Army rifle I recently saw advertised here in California by a sporting goods chain as freely available as a common shotgun. It's insanity for military-style assault weapons to be cheaper and more easily obtainable than an American-made hunting rifle.

Laws with teeth are needed

Right now, there may be laws against converting semiautomatic assault weapons into fully automatic ones. But they're doing nothing to deter the gun nuts who sell that technology on the Internet. For President Clinton's ban to be meaningful, it needs to be backed up by laws with real teeth: long prison terms for people who violate the laws we have, for those who take gun culture fantasy and turn it into fully automatic reality.

12

Law-Abiding Citizens Have a Right to Own Assault-Type Rifles

Joe Zychik

Joe Zychik is a writer and counselor based in Southern California. He is not affiliated with the NRA. He can be reached through www.armthepeople.com and www.zychik.com.

The Second Amendment ensures that the American right of self-defense cannot be infringed by the government. Therefore, Americans have the right to own so-called assault weapons. Moreover, the ban on assault weapons is essentially useless, since no one has owned true assault weapons since machine guns were outlawed in 1934. The firearms included in the assault weapons ban are no different from semiautomatic handguns that fire one shot at a time. The government has lied to the American people about guns in the hopes that they will voluntarily give up their firearms.

Should every person be able to take advantage of the best means of self-defense available? Should the President be protected by assault weapons? Should soldiers have the best firepower at their disposal? Should the police be fully equipped to handle riots and heavily armed criminals? Is your life worth as much as the President's? As a soldier's? As a police officer's?

The Founding Fathers' answer to the question of "What is the worth of an individual life?" was to write the Second Amendment, guaranteeing that your right to self-defense would not be infringed.

Why does anybody need an assault weapon? Why do you need to protect your life and your family? The answer to either question answers them both: Because you have a right to, just as you have a right to exist.

A more informed question is: Does anyone own an assault weapon? The fact-based answer is that almost no one owns an assault weapon. Since the Machine Gun Act of 1934, private ownership of assault weapons has been almost completely eliminated because an assault weapon is a portable machine gun. A machine gun, as you probably know, fires as long as your finger is on the trigger, as does an assault weapon. However, the guns that the media refer to today as assault weapons cannot fire for as long as your finger is on the trigger. The so-called assault weapons the media refer to fire the same way a semi-automatic handgun does, one shot at a time, one trigger squeeze at a time.

The belief that assault weapons have flooded the streets of America is a myth, the same kind of myth that claimed that if you kissed someone without using a mouth guard you could get AIDS, the same kind of idiocy that said cigarettes were healthier for you than candy because cigarettes helped you lose weight, and the same kind of absurdity that forced a raped woman to prove she had not asked for it.

Why does anybody need an assault weapon? . . . Because you have a right to [own one], just as you have a right to exist.

A semi-automatic rifle is not an assault weapon just as a needle and thread is not a sewing machine. With needle and thread you sew one stitch at a time just as you fire one bullet at a time with a semi-automatic rifle. A sewing machine enables you to stitch automatically just as an assault weapon enables you to defend your life and your family's with one squeeze of the trigger. The real question is not who needs an assault weapon. The real question is why were you misinformed?

Misinformed by the media

But first let us find out how misinformed you were. How often has the media told you 99.4% of all guns are not used in crimes? Why hasn't the media told you that since 1934 there have been approximately 20,000 gun control laws passed and crime has gone up? Why did the media turn its back on the Lott study which proved conclusively that rape, murder, and assault occur more frequently in areas where the citizens are denied the right of self-defense than in areas where citizens are allowed to carry concealed weapons? Why hasn't the media compared the Los Angeles riots, in which 58 people were killed, and the aftermath of Hurricane Andrew, which caused far more damage, but no one was killed by rioters or looters? Could it be that in Los Angeles it is almost impossible to get a concealed carry permit and the city's culture is anti-gun, whereas in Florida people are allowed to carry concealed weapons and citizens were able to protect their property and their lives by being heavily armed? Why doesn't the media tell you about the store owners and citizens who saved their lives, their families' lives and their property during the LA riots by using so-called assault weapons? Could it be a black out? Could it be the same kind of reporting that equates a needle and thread with a sewing machine?

You have been lied to for the same reason people want you to believe that censorship will make America a better place to live. You have been lied to for the same reason people want you to believe that it is perfectly okay for customs agents to strip search you anytime they want to. You have been lied to for the same reason people want you to believe your tax money is not being wasted, and that Social Security will provide for your retirement.

You have been lied to because certain people in the media and the government want you to voluntarily give up your rights. These people know that if they tell you the truth about assault weapons, if they tell you the truth about your right to self-defense, you will not give up that right.

The question is not who needs an assault weapon.

The question is how many of your rights are you willing to surrender to people who have lied to you?

13

Regulating Gun Show Sales Would Reduce Crime

Kristen Rand

Kristen Rand is the director of federal policy at the Violence Policy Center, an educational foundation that conducts research on firearms violence.

Gun shows provide a readily available source of weapons and ammunition—legal and illegal—for criminals and others who are prohibited from buying firearms. Gun shows are virtually unregulated, are a prime source for criminal gun traffickers, and function as a meeting place for criminals and pro-gun fringe extremists. The most effective way to reduce illegal activity at gun shows is to ban shows entirely. If a total ban is not feasible, other restrictions on buying and selling weapons at gun shows could be enacted to further reduce the shows' role in criminal gun trafficking.

In 1986 the National Rifle Association (NRA) unveiled the "Firearms Owners' Protection Act." Commonly known as "McClure-Volkmer" for its congressional sponsors, then-Senator James McClure (R-ID) and former Representative Harold Volkmer (D-MO), it was designed to roll back broad sections of the Gun Control Act of 1968 (GCA). Early versions of the bill even removed restrictions on the mail-order sale of firearms. (Throughout this executive summary and the full study the bill and law are referred to as McClure-Volkmer.)

The gun-sellers' relief act

The NRA and the bill's supporters portrayed McClure-Volkmer as a gun owners' relief act. In reality, the bill did much more to advance the interests of gun *sellers*—both Federal Firearms License (FFL) holders and unlicensed individuals—than those of the average gun owner.

After a long, bitter debate that pitted the NRA and the firearms industry against gun control advocates and national police organizations, McClure-Volkmer passed both houses of Congress and was signed into law by President Reagan on May 19, 1986. McClure-Volkmer:

Reprinted from Kristen Rand, Executive Summary of the Violence Policy Center's 1996 study *Gun Shows in America: Tupperware® Parties for Criminals,* with permission.

- Allowed Federal Firearms License holders to sell guns at gun shows located in their home state.
- Allowed individuals not federally licensed as gun dealers to sell their personal firearms as a "hobby."
- Restricted the ability of the Bureau of Alcohol, Tobacco and Firearms (ATF) to conduct inspections of the business premises of federally licensed firearms dealers.
- Reduced the recordkeeping required of federally licensed firearms dealers, specifically eliminating recordkeeping of ammunition sales.
- Raised the burden of proof for violations of federal gun laws.
- Expanded a federal program that restored the ability of convicted felons to possess firearms.

Despite the controversy generated by McClure-Volkmer, little attention has been paid to its effect in the 10 years since the law's enactment. *Gun Shows in America: Tupperware® Parties for Criminals* is the first in a series of studies in which the Violence Policy Center (VPC) will analyze the real-world impact of the NRA's McClure-Volkmer legislation and gauge the law's effect on public safety.

The legacy of McClure-Volkmer

One legacy of McClure-Volkmer is the uncontrolled proliferation of gun shows—events at which private citizens and federally licensed gun dealers congregate to buy and sell firearms and related paraphernalia. The VPC's research reveals that the law has resulted in a dramatic increase in the number and size of shows, which occur in auditoriums, fairgrounds, and other outlets in almost every state on virtually every weekend of the year. The VPC's research also reveals that this dramatic increase is due largely to two little-noticed changes McClure-Volkmer made in the way that federally licensed firearms dealers are regulated:

- The law made it legal for Federal Firearms License holders to sell at gun shows.
- The law expanded the opportunities for private citizens to buy and sell firearms at gun shows by raising the threshold of what constituted being "engaged in the business" of selling firearms.

The result is a readily available source of weapons and ammunition for a wide variety of criminals—including street gangs, white supremacists, would-be presidential assassins, and domestic terrorists.

Changes seen at gun shows as the result of McClure-Volkmer

As the result of McClure-Volkmer, hundreds of thousands of Federal Firearms License (FFL) holders previously prohibited from selling at gun shows could now do so. And "hobbyists"—those without Federal Firearms Licenses—selling from their "personal collections" could operate at gun shows with little fear of prosecution for dealing in firearms without a license.

The Bureau of Alcohol, Tobacco and Firearms (ATF) maintains no historical records as to the number of gun shows that occur annually and can only offer rough estimates as to the number today. ATF estimates that there are now 2,000 gun shows held in the United States each year. Yet, in contrast, the National Association of Arms Shows estimates there are more than 100 gun shows every weekend—for an annual total of 5,200 shows. The National Association of Arms Shows also estimates that more than five million people attend such shows each year and that they generate billions of dollars in sales.

> *Extensive evidence does exist that [gun shows] are virtually unregulated, are a key tool for criminal gun traffickers, and function as a common meeting place for criminals.*

To gauge the increase in the number of gun shows and the role of McClure-Volkmer, the Violence Policy Center conducted interviews across the country with federal, state, and local law enforcement officials as well as with gun show promoters. The VPC surveyed a total of 25 individuals in 16 states regarding their experience with gun shows and similar events, such as flea markets. Of those surveyed, 14 offered opinions on whether the number of gun shows in their area had increased or decreased. Ten of the 14—or 71 percent—stated that there had been an increase in the number of gun shows over the past 10 years. Three believed the number of shows had remained constant, and only one said the number had decreased. One regional ATF official queried additional supervisors regarding the number of gun shows in states under the office's jurisdiction and reported that "several out of my eight supervisors said we definitely had an increase of more than 50 percent in the last 10 years."

The survey found significant evidence that the changes resulting from McClure-Volkmer were a key factor in the increase in the number of gun shows and that this expansion presented federal, state, and local law enforcement officials with an array of new problems related to illegal firearms trafficking. While the exact number of shows remains uncertain, extensive evidence does exist that they are virtually unregulated, are a key tool for criminal gun traffickers, and function as a common meeting place for criminals.

A sample of the comments from law enforcement personnel and gun show promoters attest to dramatic increases in the number of gun shows during the past 10 years:

> There's a big increase in the number of gun shows. [T]here are many more than 10 years ago. Dealers can now legally sell at gun shows. Most of them, before it was legal, did not sell at shows. They're [gun shows] popular because they can increase their business. *Howard Wolfe, Area Supervisor, ATF North Atlantic District Office, Pittsburgh, PA.*

> There's more and more people with licenses becoming involved. . . . There seems to be more shows than ever before. . . . It's a fad, just like *Friends. Albert Ross, Spokesperson, Dallas Arms Collectors Association, Arlington, TX.*

Show size ranges from 150 to 1,500 tables. . . . Attendance at a good show will run seven to eight people per table at the show. I heard about a show a couple [of] weeks ago that had 18,000 people come. That's a lot of folks in two days. *David Cook, Show Organizer, North Texas Gun Club, Dallas, TX.*

"No one wants to wait"

Problems arose almost immediately when Federal Firearms License holders were allowed to sell at gun shows in direct competition with unlicensed "hobbyists" and "collectors." Licensed dealers are required to follow sales criteria under federal law: e.g., federal sales forms, age restrictions, and more recently background checks and waiting periods. Unlicensed sellers—who as private citizens did not have to meet these requirements—made a more appealing sales outlet to both the law-abiding (who, like most Americans, prefer not to wait) and the criminal purchaser seeking to avoid a paper trail. Gun show promoters, who had previously only dealt with part-time, unlicensed hobbyists, were sometimes not swift enough in familiarizing themselves with the applicable federal, state, and local laws.

Tension also grew among license holders, who are themselves divided into two groups: "storefront" or "stocking" dealers who sell from traditional retail outlets open during standard business hours, and "kitchen-table" dealers who operate out of their homes or at gun shows.

In some cases the seller does not know that the weapon is being passed on to an illegal buyer, but in others the seller is aware of the straw sale.

Bill Bridgewater, executive director of the National Alliance of Stocking Gun Dealers, expressed the sentiments of many stocking dealers in a May 1993 letter to the House of Representatives Crime and Criminal Justice Subcommittee:

The BATF has established rules and regulations for these things they call "gun shows." The opportunity for the black marketeers is that the BATF doesn't enforce those regulations and there isn't anyone else to do so. Consequently, there are literally hundreds of "gun shows" scattered around the country where you may rent tables, display your wares, sell what you please to whomever you please and once again the sale that is made with no records, no questions and no papers, earns the highest sales price. . . . There are wide open "gun shows" the length and breadth of the United States, wherein anyone may do as he chooses, including buy firearms for children.

The competition between hobbyists, kitchen-table dealers, and stocking dealers helped create an atmosphere that invited illegal conduct. The result of this competition was detailed in a July 1993 investigative report by Florida's *St. Petersburg Times*. In the article Harvey Eberg, a licensed dealer at a Tampa gun show, explained why several unlicensed sellers would not provide their names to the *Times* reporter:

> "The reason most of them won't give you their names is be-cause they're breaking the law," he said loudly. "I fight it all the time. At every gun show people walk up and ask, 'Are you a dealer?'" Eberg said. If you are, "they won't deal with you," he said, and if not, "There are no receipts, no any-thing. Just the money changes hands. It's kind of frustrat-ing. . . . [Y]ou lose out. No one wants to deal with the $5 [Florida background check] charge. No one wants to deal with the paperwork. No one wants to wait."

The Violence Policy Center survey revealed widespread frustration by law enforcement personnel over their inability to regulate gun shows and ensure compliance with federal and state law. The most often cited im-pediment to enforcement is the sheer number of shows coupled with budget and manpower limitations. As San Francisco ATF Public Informa-tion Officer Ed Gleba lamented, "There are just too many gun shows and not enough agents."

This is compounded by Bureau of Alcohol, Tobacco and Firearms policies restricting the agency's regulation of gun shows. In 1979, ATF's policy regarding gun shows and flea markets limited the agency's investi-gations to "situations where there are specific allegations that significant violations have occurred and where there is reliable information that guns sold at the specific gun show or flea market have shown up in crimes of violence with some degree of regularity." In the nearly two decades since then little has changed.

Illegal trafficking at gun shows

Illegal firearm transactions at gun shows usually occur in one of three ways:
- straw purchases
- out-of-state sales
- sales from "personal" collections

Straw purchases

Straw purchases occur when a person who is not in a restricted category (the "straw man") purchases a weapon for someone who is prohibited by federal, state, or local law from purchasing or possessing a firearm. Straw men are used by criminals, minors, or others in proscribed categories to transact sales with both Federal Firearms License holders and unlicensed hobbyists. In some cases the seller does not know that the weapon is be-ing passed on to an illegal buyer, but in others the seller is aware of the straw sale.

At a 1993 hearing on federal firearms licensing before the crime sub-committee of the House Judiciary Committee, convicted criminal Edward Daily III testified that he regularly used straw purchasers to buy handguns at gun shows in Virginia. The 22-year-old Daily traded the guns for narcotics in New York City. At the hearing, then-House Crime Subcommittee Chair Charles Schumer (D-NY), who has played a leading role in documenting gun show abuses, questioned Daily as to the role gun shows play in criminal trafficking. Daily testified, "At each gun show, there were about, maybe 250 tables with different gun dealers, and we would visit maybe 20, 30 tables. Some of them saw me every weekend, and they knew me. . . . 'Hi. How's it going. . . . Are you picking up any guns today?'" Representative Schumer asked Daily whether "this was always at gun shows?" Daily responded, "Always at gun shows."

Out-of-state dealers

Although federal law allows Federal Firearms License holders to sell at gun shows within their own state, FFL holders—and hobbyists—are not permitted to make out-of-state sales.

Evidence suggests that many dealers do not abide by the requirement that they sell only in their own state. This non-compliance by some dealers causes distress not only among law enforcement, but complying dealers. The National Association of Stocking Gun Dealers' Bill Bridgewater asserts that gun show violations occur all the time:

> If you can't see them, you're blind. When you go to a [North Carolina] gun show and you see every state licensee around you for 250 to 300 miles and you chat with various folk standing behind their table of handguns . . . [from Ohio, Florida, Virginia], does that give you a clue? There are a lot of [illegal sales being committed] under the color of an FFL traveling state to state every weekend and attending firearms shows and selling firearms unlawfully in those states. The principal reason they do is that at every gun show in this nation no one pays any attention to the law.

Other state law enforcement authorities have experienced similar problems with out-of-state dealers. For example, Richard Yarmy illegally sold a wide variety of weapons to New York City criminals who went by the names Wheelchair Luis, Freckle Face George, and Lightbulb. According to the New York district attorney, Yarmy was indicted for using his FFL—which he had possessed for more than 10 years—to supply guns illegally to Manhattan "drug dealers and other street criminals." Upon his arrest, New York officials called Yarmy "one of the highest volume dealers" at gun shows along the eastern seaboard. Weapons seized during the course of the investigation included assault pistols, Street Sweeper shotguns, and fully automatic firearms.

Despite the clear problems associated with Federal Firearms License holders selling at out-of-state gun shows, ATF may be preparing to shoot itself in the foot on this issue. In recent letters to Senator Fred Thompson (R-TN) and Representative James Oberstar (D-MN) obtained by the Violence Policy Center through the Freedom of Information Act, ATF has agreed to support, on condition of the inclusion of certain amendments, a measure (S. 1536 in the Senate and H.R. 659 in the House) allowing dealers to conduct business at out-of-state gun shows. [The bills did not pass.] Although some might argue that legalizing sales at out-of-state shows would only decriminalize activity already occurring and improve record-keeping of such sales, the risks clearly outweigh any potential benefit.

"Personal collections"

In defining the threshold of activity one must cross to be categorized as a "dealer," McClure-Volkmer specifically excludes a person who makes "exchanges or purchases of firearms for the enhancement of a personal collection . . . or who sells all or part of his personal collection of firearms." Therefore, private individuals selling firearms at gun shows from their "personal collections" are not required to obtain a Federal Firearms License, and as noted earlier, need not comply with the recordkeeping and reporting requirements that apply to license holders. In addition, unscrupulous dealers can thwart gun control laws by transferring weapons to relatives' or friends' "personal collections," to be resold with no record of the ultimate purchaser.

Where the famous and the infamous shop

Gun shows appeal to a wide range of firearm enthusiasts—from hunters and collectors looking for bargains to anti-government militia members preparing for battle against the New World Order. One show organizer characterized attendees as "the same kind of people [you find] at malls" and noted that the shows were a popular destination for local celebrities, from sports heroes to politicians.

An organizer for the North Texas Gun Club lists singer Mel Torme and members of the Dallas Cowboys as visitors to his shows. And gun shows appear to be a favored forum for political candidates in conservative locales.

Many dealers do not abide by the requirement that they sell only in their own state.

Probably the most famous politician with an affinity for gun shows is [former] presidential candidate Pat Buchanan, who prior to the March 1996 Arizona primary attended a Phoenix gun show in black cowboy shirt and hat. Urging his supporters to "take back the nation," the *New York Times* reported that he promised fellow gun show participants that he would protect the right to bear arms as part of his "crusade for America."

And the infamous

Gun shows hold a particular appeal for the pro-gun fringe. Militia members and other extremists attend shows not only to purchase weapons, but also to distribute anti-government materials and recruit new members.

In 1980 ATF Director G.R. Dickerson warned of the role gun shows had played in supplying weapons to a wide range of criminals—from the Symbionese Liberation Army to would-be presidential assassin Sara Jane Moore. The Weather Underground and the Black Liberation Army were also listed as having acquired firearms at gun shows. Two decades later, only the names have changed.

As early as 1993 the FBI, ATF, and Arizona Department of Public Safety were warned that Oklahoma City bombing suspect Timothy McVeigh's activities at a gun show raised suspicions that he might be dangerous and warranted investigation. [McVeigh was convicted in 1997 and sentenced to death for the 1995 bombing that killed 168 people.]

In June 1995, *ABC World News Tonight* reported that Timothy McVeigh's Army friend Michael Fortier had allegedly admitted to joining McVeigh and Terry Nichols in a $60,000 robbery of an Arkansas gun collector's ranch in which 70 shotguns, rifles, and handguns were taken. *ABC World News Tonight* reported that Fortier had admitted taking many of the weapons to Kingman, Arizona, and later selling them at gun shows.

Like his alleged avenger McVeigh, Branch Davidian leader David Koresh frequented gun shows. The *St. Petersburg Times* reported that Koresh purchased a large quantity of the weapons stockpiled at Mount Carmel (the Branch Davidian compound in Waco, Texas) from Hewitt Handguns, a Texas gun dealership operated by Karen Kilpatrick with Henry McMahon. Koresh had picked up their business card at a Texas gun show. Hewitt Handguns' licensed place of business was McMahon's home, and the *Times* reported that Kilpatrick and McMahon "did business mostly on weekends traveling from gun show to gun show." According to the *Times*, from 1990 to 1992, Kilpatrick and McMahon sold Koresh approximately 225 guns and 100,000 rounds of ammunition. The article noted, "Until someone told federal agents they were arming a cult leader, they reported these sales to nobody. By law, they were not required to do so."

Gun shows hold a particular appeal for . . . militia members and other extremists [who] attend shows not only to purchase weapons, but also to distribute anti-government materials and recruit new members.

In testimony before the 1995 House Judiciary Committee during hearings investigating federal actions at Waco, author Dick Reavis asserted that Koresh not only was a buyer at gun shows—he was a seller. Reavis testified that "in late 1991 he [Koresh] began buying guns and studying armaments. . . . Within a few months, Koresh and a handful of associates were not only buying but also selling goods at the shows."

The militia movement

In the 1990s, festering anti-government hysteria received validation from the National Rifle Association. The NRA bombarded gun owners with direct mail calling federal law enforcement personnel "jackbooted thugs" and warning readers that it was only a matter of time before President Clinton "pushes legislation that takes away from our freedoms and creates a police state."

With the NRA providing the motive, gun shows offered the means for disaffected gun owners to get involved with the militia movement.

William Pierce—author of the *Turner Diaries*, the "Bible" of the militia movement—has observed that "gun shows provide a natural recruiting environment. Many more are being held now than ever before, and many more people are attending them."

Gun shows are not only a key source for firearms and other material, but are a town square where extremists can gather information, make contacts, and mingle with the like-minded.

As anti-government activity by militias and other extremists has grown, so has the awareness that gun shows are not only a key source for firearms and other material, but are a town square where extremists can gather information, make contacts, and mingle with the like-minded. Gun shows are often nothing less than Tupperware® parties for criminals.

The importance of gun shows to the militia movement can be seen in the *Free Militia's Field Manual: Principles Justifying the Arming and Organizing of a Militia*. In a section on "Secrecy and Security in the Free Militia," readers are warned that "gun show" is one of the 21 "topics and words you should stay away from when talking openly in public or on the phone."

In the December 1995 *Arkansas Democrat-Gazette*, Dan S.—an undercover investigative journalist who had been an infiltrator in the extremist movement for 12 years—spoke about the role of gun shows for the militia movement:

> Another gateway into the militia subculture, which leaped into the spotlight after the Oklahoma City bombing, was the nation's vast meshwork of gun shows with its thriving commerce in weapons, paramilitary paraphernalia and anti-government invective. "Gun shows are huge in the movement," Dan acknowledged. "They're very popular in the heartland, and you can't go into one without getting the literature. They're a key dissemination point."

"Truck loads of parts are readily available"

Gun shows have also become a primary source for military hardware stolen from U.S. military installations. This has become prevalent enough to be addressed in the mainstream publications of the firearms industry. An article in the March/April 1996 issue of *Shooting Sports Retailer* asked the question, "Are gun dealers in trouble?" The article noted a shift in gun show fare from antiques and collectibles to military parts:

> In their infancy, gun shows were usually a place to go when looking for antique and collectable firearms. Some of them are still that way. But many modern gun shows seem to be more "military armory" than "old west," and a growing number of sellers are non-store dealers.

In November 1993, the Senate Committee on Governmental Affairs conducted a hearing, "Gun Violence: Do Stolen Military Parts Play a Role?" The hearing explored the findings of a November 1993 report from the Government Accounting Office (GAO), *Small Arms Parts: Poor Controls Invite Widespread Theft.* The GAO report had been undertaken at the request of Senator John Glenn (D-OH), then-chairman of the committee, to investigate reports of inadequate control by the Department of Defense over its inventory of small arms parts. The GAO found that these deficiencies allowed large-scale theft and that the stolen material was widely available at gun shows across the country. GAO personnel were able to purchase stolen military parts at gun shows in each of the six states they visited, and at 13 of the 15 gun shows they visited. At almost every gun show, GAO staff also found 30-round M-16 magazine clips in government packaging. In five states, GAO personnel were able to purchase all of the parts necessary to convert a semiautomatic AR-15 assault rifle into a fully automatic M-16 machine gun.

Stolen [military small arms parts were] widely available at gun shows across the country.

The Committee on Governmental Affairs hearing delved into who purchases stolen military parts and how the parts are filtered into the general—and often criminal—population. Michael Vaughn, detective supervisor for the Los Angeles Police Department and a witness at the Senate hearing, confirmed that many of these weapons and parts are available at gun shows:

> We recently monitored a gun show where enough parts can be purchased to assemble the M-16 automatic rifle and Colt M-1911 .45 caliber semiautomatic pistol, as well as bombs and booby traps. Many of these parts are still packaged in military crates, original Cosmoline packaging, and available in unbelievable quantities. Virtually truck loads of parts are readily available for purchase. When you go to these gun shows or you travel to swap meets, you can virtually see just about any military hardware available.

Recommendations

The dangers and problems associated with gun shows were well known in 1986 when Congress voted to pass McClure-Volkmer. Yet in spite of this, the National Rifle Association and its congressional supporters moved to pass a measure that would increase the number of gun shows and create a raft of new law enforcement problems, above and beyond the well-documented problems that already existed. To argue that the bill's effects could not have been predicted is not credible. The most cursory reading reveals that McClure-Volkmer was certain to multiply the number of gun shows and the number of people allowed to participate in them.

The most effective approach to remedying the law enforcement problems presented by gun shows would be to ban them. Gun shows could be effectively banned by reinstating the prohibition forbidding dealers to sell from any location other than their licensed place of business and requiring that all sales by a private individual be consummated by a licensed dealer. Short of banning gun shows, many restrictions and requirements could be imposed to greatly reduce the shows' role in criminal gun trafficking.

On the federal level

• Limit gun show participation to licensed dealers and step up enforcement of all existing requirements regarding posting of license, record-keeping, etc. This would eliminate confusion regarding which sellers must complete the federal paperwork and abide by waiting periods and background checks and would address the problem of licensees competing with non-licensees by engaging in illegal transactions.

• Require that Federal Firearms License holders who participate at gun shows must notify ATF when they engage in business away from their licensed premises, and require that the location and date of the gun show and number and types of guns sold at the show be reported to ATF. (This requirement could likely be promulgated by ATF under current law.)

• To facilitate the tracing of firearms transferred at gun shows, require that all firearm sales at gun shows be recorded on a separate version of the federal Form 4473. The form should include the name, location, and date of the gun show. (This requirement could likely be instituted by ATF administratively.)

• Amend the definition of "engaged in the business" to close the loophole that allows sales from a personal collection in supposed "pursuit of a hobby." One option could be to disallow such sales at gun shows altogether.

• Grant ATF interim powers such as license suspension, civil penalties, or offers of monetary settlement. Currently, ATF's enforcement tools are limited to either revoking or failing to renew a license.

• Limit the type of weapons sold at gun shows. Prohibitions on the sale of assault weapons, handguns, and weapons regulated under the National Firearms Act (e.g. machine guns, silencers, sawed-off rifles and shotguns), would reduce the shows' appeal to criminals and illegal traffickers.

• Strictly enforce the prohibitions on the sale of U.S. military hardware at gun shows. In this area, gun show organizers and promoters could play a key role in reducing distribution outlets for stolen military material. Stepped up surveillance of shows by local, state, and federal law enforcement targeting the sale of stolen military hardware is called for.

On the state or local level

• State or local authorities could require that all sales made by private individuals at gun shows be reported to local law enforcement agencies on a standardized form.

• Communities could limit the number of gun shows held in their areas. Reducing the volume of shows occurring each year would aid enforcement authorities and reduce the opportunity for criminal trafficking.

• State and local authorities could also require certification of gun show organizers and promoters. Requirements could include: keeping accurate records of all gun show participants selling firearms; showing proof that the organization carries adequate theft and liability insurance; and, showing proof that adequate steps are being taken to ensure that all sellers are complying with applicable federal, state, and local laws.

• As on the federal level, the type of weapons sold at gun shows could be limited by a state or community. Prohibitions on the sale of assault weapons, handguns, and weapons regulated under the National Firearms Act (e.g. machine guns, silencers, sawed-off rifles and shotguns), would help reduce the shows' appeal to criminals and illegal traffickers.

14

Regulating Gun Shows Is an Unreasonable Restriction on Law-Abiding Citizens

Wayne R. LaPierre

Wayne R. LaPierre is the executive vice president of the National Rifle Association.

Requiring mandatory instant background checks on purchasers at gun shows is a reasonable action to take to prevent prohibited persons—such as criminals, the mentally ill, and juveniles—from acquiring guns illegally. However, allowing the government to intrude on these private transactions—whether at a gun show, gun store, shooting range, or an inheritance—by taxing and compiling records of the transactions is unreasonable. Before the government passes new laws regulating gun shows, it should fully enforce the laws that currently regulate gun usage and ownership.

Editor's Note: In the aftermath of the shooting at the Columbine High School in Littleton, Colorado, in April, 1999, in which two teenage boys shot and killed twelve students, a teacher, and then themselves, Congress held hearings on an amendment sponsored by Senator Frank Lautenberg of New Jersey which would require all gun buyers at gun shows to undergo a background check and the sales to be registered, similar to sales at gun shops. Despite initial strong support for the amendment, it did not pass.

M y adult life has been almost entirely devoted to understanding and vindicating the Second Amendment to our Constitution. The individual, personal freedom to choose to lawfully own a firearm—without permission from, or apology to, anyone—is as clear and intentional as the rest of the Bill of Rights.

Our freedoms are already endangered enough by those who oppose them. But I've learned that a freedom is most at risk when it's in the

Reprinted from Wayne R. LaPierre, testimony before the U.S. House of Representatives Committee on the Judiciary, Subcommittee on Crime, May 27, 1999.

hands of honest people who think, for some perceived common good, they ought to give it up.

Today we are a country in shock, still bewildered by what confluence of forces could possibly lead young people to hurt each other.

In that tender state, good people are vulnerable. They want to do something, anything, for the common good. Indeed, some are so perplexed about what to do that legislators admit from the outset that their legislation could not have prevented the very crimes that provoked drafting it.

That's the very definition of a perceived, but fictitious, common good.

As this made-for-TV lawmaking gets played out, it needs a villain. So good Americans have been exposed daily to a well-coordinated systematic bashing of the National Rifle Association's membership as somehow a reckless societal pathogen, a mighty extremist empire opposed to safety, caution, and reason.

A cruel and dangerous lie

That is a cruel and dangerous lie.

Because nobody—nor any combination of entities you care to add up—has invested even a measurable fraction of what we have invested toward keeping safety and sanity central to the lawful exercise of the Second Amendment.

And nobody is more committed than we are to keeping guns out of criminals' hands. That's obviously in our best interest. It's just whether you believe you're more likely to keep guns and criminals apart with new laws you write and ignore, or with existing laws you enforce.

What is reasonable

Some think our insistence on enforcement is unreasonable. Others say we oppose reasonable restrictions on gun ownership. So let's talk about what's reasonable and what's not.

We think it's reasonable to provide mandatory instant criminal background checks for every sale at every gun show. No loopholes anywhere for anyone. That means closing the Hinckley loophole so the records of those adjudicated mentally ill are in the system.

> *We think it's reasonable to provide mandatory instant criminal background checks for every sale at every gun show.*

This isn't new, or a change of position, or a concession. I've been on record on this point consistently, from our national meeting in Denver, to paid national ads and position papers, to news interviews and press appearances. But I've repeatedly emphasized that this Administration must stop illegally keeping records of lawful gun buyers.

In fact, it's the media's well-kept secret that the NRA was an early architect and supporter of the National Instant Check System now in place.

Congressman McCollum knows we worked with him on instant checks more than a decade ago.

What is unreasonable

We think it's reasonable to provide for instant checks at gun shows just like at gun stores and pawn shops. But what's unreasonable is how the proposed Lautenberg legislation ignores the 250,000 prohibited people like felons who've walked away from gun stores—instead of being prosecuted for a federal felony for trying to buy a gun.

We think it's reasonable to prevent all juveniles convicted of violent felonies from owning guns, for life. What's unreasonable is how Lautenberg can prevent your law-abiding son from inheriting his grandpa's shotgun collection because Lautenberg classifies him as a gun show dealer who must be federally regulated.

We think it's reasonable to prosecute more than just two dozen thugs last year for putting illegal guns in criminals' hands. What's unreasonable is that Lautenberg considers legal guns in private hands subject to intrusive federal regulation, even in the privacy of your home.

What's unreasonable is how Lautenberg can prevent your law-abiding son from inheriting his grandpa's shotgun collection because Lautenberg classifies him as a gun show dealer who must be federally regulated.

For a century we've taught it's not just reasonable but essential to use safety locks, trigger locks, gun safes or any voluntary means appropriate to keep firearms out of the wrong hands. What's unreasonable is that Lautenberg can put you in prison just for failing to keep records on how many guns you own.

We think it's reasonable to make gun show instant checks just like gun store instant checks. What's unreasonable is how Lautenberg could define your Wal-Mart, or your uncle's skeet-shooting range, or your next-door firearms collector, or your local sporting clays competition, or any person or place with 50 or more firearms as a "gun show " subject to intrusive government regulation. That's crazy!

Harassing law-abiding citizens

We think it's reasonable to demand strict prosecution of criminal activity, whether it takes place in a big-city alleyway or small town gun show. What's unreasonable is that Lautenberg instead demands strict registration of law-abiding gun buyers, by giving the federal government the name and address, type of gun and serial number—not of criminals but of Americans deemed NOT to be criminals by the instant check!

We think it's reasonable to provide full funding for the National Instant Check System so it operates efficiently and instantly. What's unreasonable is how Lautenberg authorizes an unlimited gun tax on purchases by law-abiding citizens.

We think it's reasonable to expect our government to prosecute more than 24 hoods last year for providing guns to criminals. What's unreasonable is how Lautenberg makes everyone prosecutable if you just talk about buying or selling a gun at a gun show—even if you have no gun in your possession!

We think it's reasonable to support the federal Gun-Free School Zones Act. What's unreasonable is letting 6,000 students caught with illegal guns at school go, prosecuting only 13 of them the past two years.

We think it's reasonable to demand that when a lawful gun buyer passes the criminal background check and purchases a firearm, records of that transaction be destroyed immediately. What's unreasonable is Lautenberg's decree that we trust government bureaucrats to compile and keep names and addresses and firearm types of millions of honest, legal gun owners for no legitimate law enforcement purpose.

Full enforcement of the law

We think it's reasonable to expect full enforcement of federal firearms laws by the federal government. What's unreasonable is when the Justice Department claims that federal gun laws are for the states to enforce! Reasonable people know that a case made in state court means plea bargains, judge shopping and no mandatory minimum sentencing. Even Mayor Ed Rendell of Philadelphia knows this, even if the Justice Department does not. He said, "In state court, we average for these types of gun violations a 4-month prison sentence. The federal guidelines are 59 months in prison. That's a 5½ year difference. Incarcerating convicted felons in possession of firearms for that length of time will save lives. It will save carnage. It will save people from being maimed."

> *What's unreasonable is . . . giving the federal government the name and address, type of gun and serial number—not of criminals but of Americans deemed NOT to be criminals by the instant check!*

That's why we support Project Exile—the fierce prosecution of federal gun laws that has cut crime rates overnight the few places it's been tried. Even though this Administration resists it, we think it's reasonable because it works.

We only support what works, and our proud list is long. From Project Exile to three-strikes-you're-out, to truth in sentencing, to ten-twenty-life, to mandatory minimums—what's reasonable is what works; what's unreasonable is what doesn't work.

Unworkable and unenforceable

What's unreasonable is further erosion of privacy, further intrusion into private transactions, and further government penalizing of the law-abiding many instead of the lawbreaking few. America will not tolerate further surrender of precious freedoms in return for nothing but perceived but fictitious promises that make none of us safer.

The Lautenberg legislation is not only unreasonable, it is unworkable . . . unacceptable . . . and to our Founders who gave us the Second Amendment, unthinkable.

What's unreasonable is . . . [making] everyone prosecutable if you just talk about buying or selling a gun at a gun show—even if you have no gun in your possession!

And finally—somebody's got to say this out loud: It's reasonable for well-meaning people to convene hearings like this to find and fashion solutions. What's unreasonable is when a new level of hate rhetoric becomes acceptable because it's aimed at honest gun owners, as in the violent language of influential film-maker Spike Lee who reportedly said about NRA President Charlton Heston, "Shoot him—with a .44-caliber Bulldog." By his defiant silence, instead of the quick apology most American role models would offer, he sanctions hate and bears his share of culpability for the kind of violence this body seeks to stop.

On behalf of millions of gun owners who are NRA members, and tens of millions who are not yet, I am asking you to practice yourselves what is so readily preached to us: Be reasonable.

15

Gun Manufacturers Should Be Held Responsible for Illegal Use of Guns

Dennis Henigan

Dennis Henigan is the director of the Legal Action Project of the Center to Prevent Handgun Violence, a pro–gun control organization in Washington, D.C.

Several U.S. cities have sued gun manufacturers to recover the police and health care costs associated with gun violence. Since U.S. laws provide that companies can be held liable when people use their products illegally or commit illegal acts with them, gun manufacturers should be held liable for the danger posed by their product. By failing to provide safety locks on all firearms, gun manufacturers have made guns unreasonably dangerous. The gun industry must either make its products safer or pay its fair share of the costs to the community associated with the misuse of guns.

On Oct. 30, 1998, New Orleans became the first city to sue gun makers. Mayor Marc Morial, with the assistance of the Legal Action Project of the Center to Prevent Handgun Violence, has filed a lawsuit against the industry for designing and marketing handguns that lack basic safety features which would prevent shootings by children, teenagers and other unauthorized users. New Orleans seeks to hold the industry accountable for the cost of police, emergency and health-care services that the city pays for due to gun injuries and deaths that would be prevented if gun manufacturers were more responsible in the design of their products.

Since Oct. 30, four other cities—Chicago; Miami–Dade County, Fla.; Bridgeport, Conn.; and Atlanta—have filed lawsuits, and more are sure to follow. While some of these lawsuits follow New Orleans', citing the industry's inexcusable failure to make its products safer, others—particularly Chicago's—focus on the industry's negligent distribution and marketing practices that contribute to a massive illegal gun market.

Although the gun industry claims these lawsuits have no legal merit, it seeks to prevent the courts from deciding the matter. Its longtime front group, the National Rifle Association, or NRA, is pushing for special legislative protection to ensure that judges and juries never hear these cases. A bill which creates immunity from liability exclusively for the gun industry has been enacted in Georgia. A Florida bill would make the mayor of Miami–Dade County a felon for continuing his lawsuit. Other state legislatures are considering similar bills.

Not content to stop there, Georgia Republican Rep. Bob Barr, a board member of the NRA, has introduced a bill that would limit lawsuits against the industry by local governments and private citizens. Like the state bills, Barr's bill is a patent attempt to intimidate mayors and others who seek to hold the gun industry accountable for its unnecessarily dangerous products and irresponsible marketing practices. [The bill has not passed.]

The gun industry's arguments

What possibly could justify legislative action to block these lawsuits? The gun lobby's arguments reveal a remarkable ignorance of basic principles of American tort law. First, the lobby's spokespeople have argued that gun manufacturers cannot be liable unless their products don't work. According to this argument, only the gun owner whose gun doesn't shoot straight can sue a gun manufacturer. This simply is not true. According to long-accepted principles of product-liability law, a product can be defective in design regardless of whether it malfunctions.

The Ford Motor Co., for example, was liable for fires caused by the placement of its Pinto fuel tank. Even though the fuel tank did not cause the car to malfunction, the placement of the tank created an unreasonable risk that passengers would be incinerated following a collision. Similarly, the failure of gun manufacturers to install safety devices to prevent gun accidents makes guns unreasonably dangerous even if they reliably shoot bullets.

Second, the industry also claims that it cannot be liable because its products are legal. This argument confuses criminal liability, which applies only to illegal conduct, with civil liability, which does not. Most of civil tort law concerns the liability of parties whose actions, though they may be legal, nevertheless are irresponsible and expose others to unreasonable risk of harm. Ford's placement of the Pinto gas tank did not violate any statute, but it created a significant hazard for which Ford was liable.

The law should punish the criminal who uses the gun, but it should not immunize an industry if it fails to take reasonable steps to ensure that criminals cannot misuse the gun.

Moreover, people (and companies) whose conduct violated no law can be held liable for increasing the risk that someone else will act illegally. In 1997, the Florida Supreme Court ruled unanimously that Kmart was liable for selling a rifle to an intoxicated buyer who then shot his girlfriend. Kmart's sale of the gun violated no statute but was so irresponsible that the company was held answerable for the harm caused. Saying that an industry's practices violated no statutes is no defense.

Third, the gun industry also confidently asserts that it cannot be liable when its products are misused by others. If we adhered to this principle generally, we never would have held auto manufacturers liable for selling cars without seat belts and other safety features because most car accidents are caused by driver error.

The law wisely imposes a duty on manufacturers to do what they can to reduce the risk of foreseeable injury, even when the wrongful conduct of another is a more direct cause of the harm. Recently, the Ohio Supreme Court held that the maker of a disposable lighter may be liable for failing to use feasible means to protect against misuse by children. The court wrote: "[A] product may be found defective in design . . . where the manufacturer fails to incorporate feasible safety features to prevent harm caused by foreseeable human error." That is precisely the basis for the New Orleans lawsuit: Because the gun industry is well aware that many gun owners make the mistake of leaving guns accessible to children who then misuse them, it should be liable for its failure to use feasible safety systems to prevent this foreseeable, and tragic, misuse of its products. And, as Kmart learned, gun sellers can be liable even when the misuse is criminal.

Holding companies liable for increasing the risk of injury from misuse does not shift the blame away from other culpable parties. It makes all parties who contributed to the harm responsible for their conduct.

Guns, unlike any other consumer product, are exempt from regulation by the Consumer Product Safety Commission.

The law should punish the reckless driver but not immunize the automaker who could have made the car safer. The law should punish the criminal who uses the gun, but it should not immunize an industry if it fails to take reasonable steps to ensure that criminals cannot misuse the gun. And we are not talking simply about the criminal use of guns. The gun industry is shockingly indifferent to the suicides and unintentional shootings that could be averted if they included basic safety features which would prevent children from using them. When the industry markets guns with so little trigger resistance that a 2-year-old can fire them, why should the blame rest only on the toddler and on the parents who made the gun accessible? Gun manufacturers have the capability to prevent these tragedies from happening. Why should they escape all accountability for failing to do so?

A disingenuous argument

The gun lobby insists that these lawsuits are an improper use of the courts to resolve issues that should be decided by state legislatures. If we want to change the way guns are designed and sold, this argument goes, then such changes should be made by legislatures, not courts. If this argument justifies blocking lawsuits against the gun industry, then it would apply to other industries as well. Yet, the courts did not dismiss the liability lawsuits against Ford on the grounds that the only remedy for victims of exploding Pintos was to seek greater safety regulation of autos from Congress.

This argument is simply disingenuous. The gun industry hardly would support greater regulation imposed by Congress. The industry always has resisted any kind of reform.

The gun industry conducts itself without regard for public safety precisely because it bears none of the costs of that conduct.

One purpose of product-liability law is to encourage manufacturers to increase product safety. This is particularly compelling in the case of firearms. Guns, unlike any other consumer product, are exempt from regulation by the Consumer Product Safety Commission. Having used its lobbying clout to protect itself from safety standards, the gun industry now seeks to shield itself from accountability to those injured by its conduct.

The industry's argument of last resort is that the lawsuits are nothing more than greedy lawyers seeking to extort legal fees by threatening a legitimate industry. This argument mimics the response of every industry under legal attack for selling unreasonably dangerous products. It essentially amounts to a strategy of changing the subject. Finding it difficult to defend its conduct, the gun industry makes an issue of the lawyers attacking it.

Of course, the lawyers for the cities will receive contingency fees (a percentage of any award) only if these lawsuits are successful. In contrast, the defense lawyers for the gun industry, who are paid hundreds of dollars per hour, will be paid regardless of whether the industry is vindicated.

The costs to society

The gun industry is a relatively small one that inflicts huge costs on society. Annual sales estimates run anywhere from $1.7 billion to $9 billion. Meanwhile, direct and indirect costs of gun violence amount to more than $23 billion a year, most of which is borne by taxpayers. Given that much of these costs are the result of shootings the industry could prevent, the industry's irresponsibility effectively is being subsidized by taxpayers. Why should this subsidy be allowed to continue?

The gun industry conducts itself without regard for public safety precisely because it bears none of the costs of that conduct. Although it would be entirely fair to shift those costs, the primary purpose of these lawsuits is not to recover damages but to change the way the industry does business.

The mayors who already have filed lawsuits and those who are considering filing are not going to be intimidated by the legislation proposed by Barr. It is not these lawsuits which are frivolous, but his legislation, which grants exclusive immunity to gun manufacturers and denies these mayors and private citizens the fundamental right to be heard in a court of law.

The gun industry has a choice: It can continue business as usual, but only if it pays its fair share of the cost, or it can take the necessary and feasible steps to reduce the misuse of its products by children and criminals. For creating this dilemma for the gun industry, the mayors should be praised, not condemned.

16

Gun Manufacturers Should Not Be Held Responsible for Illegal Use of Guns

Michael I. Krauss and Robert A. Levy

Michael I. Krauss is a law professor at George Mason University. Robert A. Levy is a senior fellow in constitutional studies at the Cato Institute, a think tank in Washington, D.C.

Lawsuits filed by cities against the gun industry are not only a dangerous way to change public policy, but also threaten the U.S. legal system. Government lawsuits against legitimate businesses are little more than a form of legal extortion. Tort law requires that in order for damages to be claimed, a product must be defective, not merely dangerous to use. The cities' real objective is to drive gun manufacturers out of business. If governments are allowed to sue industries for indirect harm, there will be nothing to prevent them from expanding their reach and suing other industries. Reforming the legal system could stop this litigation tyranny.

Hot on the heels of the carnage in Littleton, Colorado [in which two teenage boys shot and killed twelve students and a teacher in April 1999], President Clinton has proposed a grab bag of new gun-control measures—never mind that they wouldn't have stopped the Littleton murders, whose perpetrators broke a dozen laws already on the books. An unspeakable event rocks the public, and our politicians seize on the ensuing anti-gun sentiment to advance their otherwise frustrated gun-control agenda.

Lawsuits threaten the rule of law

Doubtless the same opportunism will spark a new round of litigation by mayors against the firearms industry. Already at least eight cities have filed suit—Atlanta, Bridgeport (Conn.), Chicago, Cincinnati, Cleveland, Detroit, Miami, and New Orleans—to recoup public outlays stemming from gun-related violence. Their suits are the leading edge of a novel and dangerous approach to public policy that ultimately threatens the rule of law.

When governments use the judiciary to recover "damages," the courts intrude on the regulatory and revenue responsibilities of legislatures. And when lawsuits based on tenuous legal theories impose high costs on defendants, due process gives way to a form of extortion, with public officials serving as bagmen for private contingency fee lawyers. Those lawyers, fresh from reaping billion-dollar awards representing states in their litigation against Big Tobacco, have fanned out in search of new industries to sue. Gun makers are their latest prey, and mayors their latest allies. The predictable result is growing public contempt for our legal institutions.

The cities' arguments

The eight cities suing the gun industry rely on a variety of arguments. Most of them contend that firearms are "defective and unreasonably dangerous" if sold without devices that prevent discharge by unauthorized users. These cities demand compensation for the treatment of gun-related injuries, police overtime, street cleaning after shootings, and tax revenue lost through reduced worker productivity and lower property values. Bridgeport's mayor is also contemplating a civil rights claim, on the ground that gun violence takes place in predominantly minority neighborhoods. (While 80 percent of homicide victims in Bridgeport are minorities, so are 90 percent of homicide defendants.)

When lawsuits based on tenuous legal theories impose high costs on defendants, due process gives way to a form of extortion.

The theory underlying Chicago's novel lawsuit is more radical still. The Windy City charges that the gun industry's "negligent marketing" and sales tactics create a "public nuisance" jeopardizing the health and safety of Chicagoans. Manufacturers allegedly "saturate" markets in jurisdictions whose gun laws are less restrictive than Chicago's, knowing full well that some purchasers will take their weapons into the city.

Chicago seeks damages and court orders that amount to judge-imposed gun control: an injunction forbidding sales to people who have purchased guns in the last 30 days, sales in excess of "lawful demand" (whatever that means), and sales of "firearms that by their design are unreasonably attractive to criminals." Usually, plaintiffs in lawsuits ask that defendants obey existing laws. But no existing law contains the requirements Chicago seeks to enforce. (Ironically, by the logic of "negligent marketing," New Orleans could become a defendant in Chicago's suit: Mayor Marc Morial recently approved a deal to sell 8,000 confiscated guns to commercial dealers, who in turn resell them throughout the Midwest, from Abilene to—you guessed it—the suburbs of Chicago.)

But simple economics puts the lie to the negligent-marketing claim. If gun makers reduce the supply of firearms sold to suburban dealers, the market price of guns will rise. Consumers with the most "elastic" demand—those who are most sensitive to price changes—will reduce or eliminate their purchases. And the evidence is clear: Price-sensitive consumers tend to be law-abiding citizens. By contrast, criminals' demand for firearms is highly "inelastic": Crooks are willing to pay inflated black-market prices for their guns. Perversely, by restricting the legal supply of guns and raising their price, plaintiffs would put more weapons in criminals' hands and fewer in the hands of honest citizens.

Perhaps most important, liability for "saturating the market" is unheard of in tort law and incompatible with a legal system based on individual responsibility. Is General Motors liable when the market for cars is "saturated" in Southern California, resulting in traffic jams and accidents? Or do motorists bear the burden of their voluntary consumption decisions, constrained only by their obligation to drive carefully?

Claiming damages for indirect harm

All eight cities' gun suits share an important characteristic of the tobacco settlements: They claim damages for *indirect* harm. The plaintiff cities do not argue that their property was hit by gunfire, only that they lost revenue when gunfire harmed others. Tort law, however, is classically based on direct harm. Suing for indirect damage flies in the face of 150 years of tort law.

The rule against indirect recovery is fundamental. Last year [1998], in *Seafarers' Welfare Plan* v. *Philip Morris,* a federal judge held that "the long-standing rule [against recovery for indirect harm] bars Plaintiffs' claims in this case, notwithstanding Plaintiffs' artful re-characterization of them" as direct. On this threshold issue alone, the cities' suits against gun makers are losers. But there's more.

To hold gun makers liable for selling an unsafe product, tort law requires that the product be truly defective, not merely dangerous. American case law has consistently rejected claims that firearms are inherently defective. Indeed, empirical data gathered by Gary Kleck, professor of criminology at Florida State University, and by John R. Lott Jr., law professor at the University of Chicago, reveal that handguns, far from being defective, in fact deter and substantially reduce violent crime when they are carried by non-felons. The lead plaintiff's counsel in the New Orleans case, Wendell Gauthier, himself carries a gun—presumably because he assigns to it greater utility than risk.

To hold gun makers liable for selling an unsafe product, tort law requires that the product be truly defective, not merely dangerous.

Then there is the public-nuisance argument. The American Law Institute, in its authoritative *Restatement of the Law Second, Torts,* defines a public nuisance as "an unreasonable interference with a right common to the general public." David Kairys of Temple University Law School, co-counsel in the Chicago case, has urged the adoption of that doctrine in

gun cases. But Kairys has it backwards. It is Chicago's lawsuit that consti-
tutes a public nuisance. The sale of guns does not violate any right common to the general public.

On the contrary, individuals have a right to protect themselves
against criminal conduct. Gun ownership, by facilitating self-defense,
helps secure that right. Wrongful behavior, not an inanimate object, is
the cause of gunshot injuries. Legitimate ownership of firearms, which
are present in almost 50 percent of American homes, cannot be a predic-
tor of violent behavior.

Guns are highly regulated

The manufacture, sale, and ownership of handguns are highly regulated.
Statutes ban certain guns. It's a federal crime for felons or drug users to
purchase or possess any firearm. It's illegal for retailers to sell handguns
to minors. Sales of more than one firearm must be reported to authorities.
Background checks of purchasers are federally mandated. Handguns are
the only consumer products for which manufacturers, wholesalers, and
retailers are all required to have federal licenses. Handguns are also the
only products that may not be purchased outside one's state of residence.
The design of every new model must be inspected and approved by the
Bureau of Alcohol, Tobacco and Firearms.

If a gun dealer knowingly condones "straw purchases" on behalf of
criminals, that dealer can be prosecuted. Curiously, not one of the retailers targeted by Chicago's undercover stings has been charged. If their behavior was as egregious as the city's complaint suggests, why have they
not been held criminally liable?

Why the lawsuits threaten the legal system

If the cases against gun manufacturers are so insubstantial, why is the litigation so threatening to the industry and to the rule of law? A number
of factors conspire to transform weak legal cases into effective means of
accomplishing a shakedown: the use of juries in civil cases, procedural
rules that make it difficult to have even lame cases dismissed prior to extensive litigation, huge potential damages, and the perverse incentives
that drive lawsuits when public officials hire private attorneys on a contingency fee basis.

Alone among Western democracies, the United States provides for juries in civil cases. That turns out to be a costly practice. Because juries
more than judges are willing to overlook legal niceties when an injured
plaintiff seeks damages from an unpopular corporate defendant, jury ver-
dicts tend to favor plaintiffs. Not only are plaintiffs more likely to prevail
if the case is heard by a jury, but they are likely to recover a larger sum as
well. Indeed, jurors can reduce their own taxes by holding defendants liable for public outlays. The effect is to make defendants more amenable
to settlement.

Procedural rules also push defendants toward settlement, even when
their case is strong on the merits. In many jurisdictions, courts are reluc-
tant to dismiss a case prior to far-reaching discovery. Thus, plaintiffs can
engage in fishing expeditions for documents that might support their

case or embarrass the defendants. Even after discovery is complete, a case typically is not dismissed without trial if there is any potentially significant factual dispute.

Yet another intimidating factor, which played a major role in the state tobacco suits, is the enormous award that could flow from an adverse verdict. When government sues a private firm to recover public expenditures, the plaintiff is not a single individual but a large class of allegedly injured parties. While a defendant might risk going to trial when a few private claimants demand relatively small sums, the stakes are greatly magnified when government is the claimant and the litigation is effectively a class action.

Last, gun makers and other industries have reason to be concerned about the unholy alliance between government and the private bar. Although the gun suits are based on different legal theories than the tobacco suits, they enjoy a common lineage. Both series of suits were concocted by a handful of private attorneys who entered into contingency fee contracts with public officials. In effect, members of the private bar were hired as government subcontractors, but with a huge financial interest in the outcome. Imagine a state attorney general corralling criminals on a contingency-fee basis, or state troopers paid per traffic stop. The potential for corruption is enormous. Most of the tobacco-suit contracts were awarded without competitive bidding to lawyers who often bankrolled state political campaigns—some of the same lawyers now vying for largesse from the mayors who are suing the gun industry.

Government is the sole entity authorized to wield coercive power against private citizens. When government functions as prosecutor or plaintiff in a legal proceeding in which it also dispenses punishment, safeguards against state misbehavior are essential. That is why we need the protections of the Fourth, Fifth, Sixth, and Eighth Amendments. That is why we demand proof beyond a reasonable doubt in criminal proceedings. That is why in civil litigation we rely primarily on private remedies, with redress sought by directly injured parties, not the state.

Wrongful behavior, not an inanimate object, is the cause of gunshot injuries.

Contingency fee contracts between governments and private attorneys should be illegal. Free societies should not condone private lawyers' enforcing public law when those lawyers have a personal stake in securing severe penalties. Legislatures or the courts should shut down this plunder by the plaintiffs' bar.

The cities' real agenda

In the quest to exact damages from gun makers, fairness and equity are not the overriding objective. Philadelphia mayor Edward G. Rendell, who first proposed simultaneous court filings by as many as 100 cities, put it this way: "The impact of so many cities' filing suit all at once would be monumental for gun manufacturers. . . . They don't have the deep pockets of the tobacco industry, and it could bring them to the negotiating table a lot sooner." Evidently the merits of the litigation are secondary to Mayor Rendell. Even frivolous litigation can bring an industry to its knees. It worked against Big Tobacco; it will work against small gun manufacturers. The Center to Prevent Handgun Violence is open and candid about its ultimate goal: "Guns must now become the next tobacco."

By the way, Mayor Rendell also claimed that cities are not after big bucks, only improved safety features and changes in distribution practices. Other mayors, however, were busily soliciting private lawyers to work for a percentage of money damages. Rendell's statement came one day after Miami filed suit seeking hundreds of millions of dollars in police, paramedic, and hospital expenses; one day after Bridgeport filed, asking $100 million in expenses stemming from gunfire; and not long after Chicago entered its claim for a whopping $433 million.

Where will it end? More kids are killed by bicycles than by guns. Will our mayors be stalking those industries?

Where will it end? More kids are killed by bicycles than by guns. Will our mayors be stalking those industries? If gun manufacturers are responsible for violence, why not sue the makers of the steel used in the guns? Why not sue match and knife manufacturers for the damage caused by arson and stabbing? Why not sue Ford when one of its dealers sells a car involved in a drunk driving fatality? If anything, gun dealers are less culpable than automobile and knife retailers, who make no effort at all to ensure that their customers are not criminals.

What we have here is a legal system run amok—social engineering without restraint and without concern for personal responsibility. Yesterday tobacco, today guns, tomorrow who knows what. The reforms of the civil justice system that would put a stop to this litigation tyranny are well established: Adopt a "loser pays" rule for legal fees, at least in civil cases where the plaintiff is the government; ban contingency fee contracts between the government and private attorneys; and bar tort suits by persons who have suffered injuries while criminally using a firearm. At a more basic level, we must stop misusing our legal machinery to strike out at bogeymen. If we don't, someday when we need it, we'll find that our legal system has been damaged beyond repair.

17

Firearm Education, Not Gun Control, Would Reduce Crime

John Michael Snyder

John Michael Snyder is the director of public affairs at the Citizens Committee for the Right to Keep and Bear Arms in Washington, D.C.

Sex education in schools has been shown to reduce sex crimes. Therefore, students should receive mandatory firearms training in order to reduce gun violence. Studies show that when gun ownership and use increase, the rates of violent crime decline. Easing restrictions on guns and training students in the safe handling of firearms will reduce violent crime and gun violence.

According to the elitist liberal establishment, mandatory sex education in schools benefits America. The more kids learn about sex from competent instructors, they say, the less sex crime there will be. The more kids learn about the intricacies of sexual intimacy, even sometimes with the use of "anatomically correct" dolls, they affirm, the fewer "unwanted pregnancies" there will be.

Gun education

So why not apply the same reasoning to youngsters and guns? The more kids learn about guns in school, the fewer "gun crimes" there will be. What America really needs, then, is *mandatory gun education* in the schools. Then you'll really see the rates of crime committed by kids with guns take a nosedive.

Let the elitists in the liberal establishment be consistent for a change. Let them avoid the allegation of public-policy schizophrenia they now face because they support sex ed in the schools on the one hand but, on the other hand, oppose the mere presence of guns on or even near school grounds.

It's gun education rather than gun prohibition that will lead to a safer social environment and preclude an explosion of gun crimes in our schools. Let boys and girls learn all about handguns, rifles, shotguns and ammunition from competent instructors in required classroom and laboratory programs. If mandatory sex ed will reduce sex crime, surely mandatory gun ed will reduce gun crime.

Actually, the outlines for full-scale national firearms handling, safety and competency programs already exist. These may be found in the "Eddie Eagle" and other youth programs developed and sponsored by the National Rifle Association. With these programs, school-age youngsters receive thorough training in the safe and efficient use of firearms.

This is not as far-fetched an approach to the youth crime and guns issue as it may seem at first glance to some people. Research demonstrates generally that laws facilitating firearm ownership and use by law-abiding citizens correlate with reductions in rates of violent crime.

The more kids learn about guns in school, the fewer "gun crimes" there will be.

Conversely, laws which restrict such activity correlate with increases, rather than decreases, in rates of violent crime. In the most recent study in this field, the book *More Guns, Less Crime*, published in 1998, University of Chicago law professor John R. Lott Jr. disputes those who supported the national five-day handgun-purchase waiting period mandated until Nov. 30, 1998, by the Brady law. "No statistically significant evidence has appeared that the Brady law has reduced crime," he writes, "and there is some statistically significant evidence that rates for rape and aggravated assault have actually risen by about 4 percent relative to what they would have been without the law."

Lott also has gathered and analyzed evidence demonstrating that the 31 states that adopted laws allowing citizens to carry concealed handguns reduced murders by 8.5 percent, rapes by 5 percent, aggravated assaults by 6 percent and robbery by 3 percent. "If the rest of the country had adopted right-to-carry concealed handgun provisions in 1992, about 1,500 murders and 4,000 rapes would have been avoided," he writes.

What the police chiefs believe

Surveys of the nation's chiefs of police and sheriffs conducted annually by the National Association of Chiefs of Police, or NACOP, suggest that America's law-enforcement command officers detect a correlation between a law-abiding armed citizenry and a safer society.

According to NACOP's 10th annual survey, mailed in 1997 to 16,000 command officers and garnering a reputable 10 percent response, 89 percent said the national five-day handgun-purchase waiting period mandated by the Brady law has not prevented criminals from obtaining firearms from illegal sources. More than 96 percent believe that any law-abiding citizen should be able to obtain a firearm for recreation or home protection. More than 93 percent believe that, since in past years riots, earthquakes, hurricanes, floods and other natural disasters have required citizens to protect themselves and their property until order could be restored, any law-abiding citizen should continue to be able to purchase any legal weapon for self-defense. More than 89 percent believe the Second Amendment to the Constitution recognizes the right of any law-abiding citizen to purchase a firearm for sport or self-defense. More than 72 percent oppose laws limiting purchases of firearms to one a month by law-abiding citizens. More than 63 percent oppose rules mandating the sales of gun locks with the sales of firearms.

The message hardly could be clearer. If America wants fewer crimes of violence, we need to eliminate restrictions on law-abiding citizens' acquisition and use of firearms and train the youngsters in our schools in the safe and efficient handling of firearms. In other words, America needs firearms education.

Organizations to Contact

The editors have compiled the following list of organizations concerned with the issues debated in this book. The descriptions are derived from materials provided by the organizations. All have publications or information available for interested readers. The list was compiled on the date of publication of the present volume; the information provided here may change. Be aware that many organizations take several weeks or longer to respond to inquiries, so allow as much time as possible.

American Civil Liberties Union (ACLU)
125 Broad St., 18th Fl., New York, NY 10004-2400
(215) 549-2500
e-mail: aclu@aclu.org • website: http://www.aclu.org

The ACLU is a national organization that works to defend Americans' civil rights as guaranteed by the U.S. Constitution. The union interprets the Second Amendment as a guarantee for states to form militias, not as a guarantee of the individual right to own and bear firearms. Consequently, the organization believes that gun control is constitutional and necessary. The ACLU publishes the semi-annual *Civil Liberties* newsletter in addition to policy statements and reports.

Citizens Committee for the Right to Keep and Bear Arms (CCRKBA)
12500 NE Tenth Pl., Bellevue, WA 98005
(425) 454-4911 • fax: (425) 451-3959
e-mail: info@ccrkba.org • website: http://www.ccrkba.org

The committee believes that the U.S. Constitution's Second Amendment guarantees and protects the right of individual Americans to own guns. It works to educate the public concerning this right and to lobby legislators to prevent the passage of gun control laws. The committee is affiliated with the Second Amendment Foundation. It publishes the books *Gun Laws of America*, *Gun Rights Fact Book*, *Origin of the Second Amendment*, and *Point Blank: Guns and Violence in America*.

Coalition to Stop Gun Violence
1000 16th St. NW, Suite 603, Washington, DC 10036
(202) 530-0340 • fax: (202) 530-0331
e-mail: noguns@aol.com • website: http://www.gunfree.org

Formerly the National Coalition to Ban Handguns, the coalition lobbies at the local, state, and federal levels to ban the sale of handguns and assault weapons to individuals. It also litigates cases against firearms makers. Its publications include various informational sheets on gun violence and the *Stop Gun Violence Newsletter* and the *Firearms Litigation Reporter*.

Doctors for Integrity in Policy Research (DIPR)
442 Diablo Rd., PMB #121, Danville, CA 94526
(925) 362-4333
e-mail: suter@dipr.org • website: http://www.dipr.org

DIPR is a national think tank of approximately five hundred medical school professors, researchers, and practicing physicians who are committed to exposing biased and incompetent research, editorial censorship, and unsound public policy. It believes that substandard science is extremely prevalent in medical literature on guns and violence. DIPR publishes the papers "Guns in Medical Literature: A Failure of Peer Review," "Assault Weapons Revisited: An Analysis of the AMA Report," and "Ammunition Registration: A Case Study of Useless Law."

Handgun Control, Inc.
1225 Eye St. NW, Suite 1100, Washington, DC 20005
(202) 898-0792 • fax: (202) 371-9615
website: http://www.handguncontrol.org

A citizens' lobby working for the federal regulation of the manufacture, sale, and civilian possession of handguns and automatic weapons, the organization successfully promoted the passage of the Brady law, which mandated a five-day waiting period for the purchase of handguns. The lobby publishes the quarterly newsletter *Progress Report* and the book *Guns Don't Die—People Do*, as well as legislative reports and pamphlets.

Independence Institute
14142 Denver West Pkwy., Suite 185, Golden, CO 80401
(303) 279-6536 • fax: (303) 279-4176
e-mail: webmngr@i2i.org • website: http://www.i2i.org

The Independence Institute is a pro–free market think tank that supports gun ownership as a civil liberty and a constitutional right. Its publications include books and booklets opposing gun control, such as *Children and Guns: Sensible Solutions, The Assault Weapon Panic: "Political Correctness" Takes Aim at the Constitution,* and *The Samurai, the Mountie, and the Cowboy: Should America Adopt the Gun Controls of Other Democracies?*

Jews for the Preservation of Firearms Ownership (JPFO)
PO Box 270143, Hartford, WI 53027
(414) 673-9745 • fax: (414) 673-9746
e-mail: jpfo@jpfo.org • website: http://www.jpfo.org

JPFO is an educational organization that believes Jewish law mandates self-defense. Its primary goal is the elimination of the belief that gun control is a socially useful public policy in any country. JPFO publishes the quarterly *Firearms Sentinel*, the comic book *"Gun Control" Kills Kids!*, and the books *Gun Control: Gateway to Tyranny* and *Lethal Laws*.

The Lawyer's Second Amendment Society, Inc. (LSAS)
18034 Ventura Blvd., No. 329, Encino, CA 91316
(818) 734-3066
e-mail: LSAS3@aol.com • website: http://www.thelsas.org

The society is a nationwide network of attorneys and others who are interested in preserving the inalienable right to keep and bear arms. It attempts to educate citizens about what it believes is their inalienable right, recognized and guaranteed by the Constitution's framers, to defend themselves with firearms, if necessary. The society publishes the *Liberty Pole* newsletter six times a year.

National Crime Prevention Council (NCPC)
1700 K St. NW, 2nd Fl., Washington, DC 20006-3817
(202) 261-4111 • fax: (202) 296-1356
e-mail: webmaster@ncpc.org • website: http://www.ncpc.org

The NCPC is a branch of the U.S. Department of Justice. It works to teach Americans how to reduce crime and addresses the causes of crime in its programs and educational materials. It provides readers with information on gun control and gun violence. The NCPC's publications include the newsletter *Catalyst*, which is published ten times a year, the book *Reducing Gun Violence: What Communities Can Do*, and the booklet *Making Children, Families, and Communities Safer from Violence*.

National Firearms Association (NFA)
Box 4384, Station C, Calgary, AB T2T 5N2 CANADA
(403) 640-1110 • (403) 640-1198 • fax: (403) 640-1144
e-mail: nfadat@telusplanet.net • website: http://www.nfa.ca

The NFA is the primary reservoir of legal and legislative expertise in the Canadian firearms community. It provides research data, expert witnesses, and education to the firearms community and others. NFA publishes the monthly newsletter *Pointblank* as well as *Canadian Hunting & Shooting, Bowhunting*, and *Angler* magazines.

National Institute of Justice (NIJ)
National Criminal Justice Reference Service (NCJRS)
Box 6000, Rockville, MD 20849
(301) 519-5500 • (800) 851-3420
e-mail: askncjrs@ncjrs.org • website: http://www.ncjrs.org

A component of the Office of Justice Programs of the U.S. Department of Justice, the NIJ supports research on crime, criminal behavior, and crime prevention. The National Criminal Justice Reference Service acts as a clearinghouse that provides information and research about criminal justice. Its publications include the research briefs "Reducing Youth Gun Violence: An Overview of Programs and Initiatives," "Impacts of the 1994 Assault Weapons Ban," and "Homicide in Eight U.S. Cities: Trends, Context, and Policy Implications."

National Rifle Association of America (NRA)
11250 Waples Mill Rd., Fairfax, VA 22030
(703) 267-1000 • fax: (703) 267-3989
website: http://www.nra.org

The NRA is America's largest organization of gun owners. It is the primary lobbying group for those who oppose gun control laws. The NRA believes that such laws violate the U.S. Constitution and do nothing to reduce crime. In addition to its monthly magazines *American Rifleman, American Hunter*, and *Incites*, the NRA publishes numerous books, bibliographies, reports, and pamphlets on gun ownership, gun safety, and gun control.

Second Amendment Foundation (SAF)
12500 NE Tenth Pl., Bellevue, WA 98005
(425) 454-7012 • (800) 426-4302 • fax: (425) 451-3959
e-mail: info@saf.org • website: http://www.saf.org

The foundation defends citizens' rights to privately own and possess firearms. It believes gun control laws violate this right. SAF maintains biographical archives and a library, copies statistics, and publishes the *Journal on Firearms and Public Policy* periodically, the *Second Amendment Reporter* quarterly, *Women and Guns* monthly, and other monographs and pamphlets.

Violence Policy Center (VPC)
1140 19th St. NW, Suite 600, Washington, DC 20036
e-mail: comment @vpc.org • website: http://www.vpc.org

The center is an educational foundation that conducts research on firearms violence. It works to educate the public concerning the dangers of guns and supports gun control measures. The center's publications include the report "Cease Fire: A Comprehensive Strategy to Reduce Firearms Violence" and the books *NRA: Money, Firepower, and Fear* and *Assault Weapons and Accessories in America*.

Bibliography

Books

Jack Anderson
Inside the NRA: Armed and Dangerous: An Exposé. New York: Dove, 1996.

Marjolijn Bijlefeld, ed.
The Gun Control Debate: A Documentary History. Westport, CT: Greenwood Press, 1997.

Marjolijn Bijlefeld
People for and Against Gun Control. Westport, CT: Greenwood Press, 1999.

John B. Bruce and Clyde Wilcox, eds.
The Changing Politics of Gun Control. Totowa, NJ: Roman and Littlefield, 1998.

Philip J. Cook, ed.
Kids, Guns, and Public Policy. Durham, NC: Duke University School of Law, 1996.

Osha Gray Davidson
Under Fire: The NRA and the Battle for Gun Control. Iowa City: University of Iowa Press, 1998.

Tom Diaz
Making a Killing: The Business of Guns in America. New York: New Press, 1999.

Jan E. Dizard, Robert Merrill Muth, and Stephen P. Andrews, eds.
Guns in America: A Reader. New York: New York University Press, 1999.

David Grossman
On Killing: The Psychological Cost of Learning to Kill in War and Society. Boston: Little, Brown, 1995.

Dennis A. Henigan, E. Bruce Nicholson, and David Hemenway
Guns and the Constitution: The Myth of Second Amendment Protection for Firearms in America. Northampton, MA: Aletheia Press, 1995.

Jacob G. Hornberger and Richard M. Ebeling, eds.
The Tyranny of Gun Control. Fairfax, VA: Future of Freedom Foundation, 1998.

Don B. Kates Jr. and Gary Kleck
The Great American Gun Debate: Essays on Firearms and Violence. San Francisco: Pacific Research Institute, 1997.

Gary Kleck
Targeting Guns: Firearms and Their Control. New York: Aldine de Gruyter, 1997.

David B. Kopel, ed.
Guns: Who Should Have Them? New York: Prometheus, 1995.

Earl R. Kruschke
Gun Control: A Reference Handbook. Santa Barbara, CA: ABC-CLIO, 1995.

John R. Lott Jr.
More Guns, Less Crime: Understanding Crime and Gun-Control Laws. Chicago: University of Chicago Press, 1998.

Joseph F. Sheley and James D. Wright	*In the Line of Fire: Youths, Guns, and Violence in Urban America*. New York: Aldine de Gruyter, 1995.
Robert J. Spitzer	*The Politics of Gun Control*. Chatham, NJ: Chatham House, 1995.
Suzanne Squyres, Jacquelyn Quiram, and Nancy R. Jacobs, eds.	*Gun Control: Restricting Rights or Protecting People?* Wylie, TX: Information Plus, 1997.
Robert A. Waters	*The Best Defense: True Stories of Intended Victims Who Defended Themselves with a Firearm*. Nashville: Cumberland House, 1998.
William Weir	*A Well Regulated Militia: The Battle over Gun Control*. North Haven, CT: Archon, 1997.

Periodicals

Massad Ayoob	"Arm Teachers to Stop School Shootings," *Wall Street Journal*, May 21, 1999.
Bob Barr	"No: Don't Let Trial Lawyers and Big-City Mayors Roll Back the Second Amendment," *Insight*, April 26, 1999. Available from 3600 New York Ave. NE, Washington, DC 20002.
Fox Butterfield	"Most Crime Guns Are Bought, Not Stolen," *New York Times*, April 30, 1999.
Dana Charry and Ellen Charry	"The Crisis of Violence," *Christian Century*, July 15–22, 1998.
Kevin Clarke	"Bang, Bang, We're Dead," *U.S. Catholic*, May 1999.
Ted Deeds	"Guns, Crime, Troubled Kids and Predatory Politicians," *Shield*, Fall 1998. Available from 7700 Leesburg Pike, #421, Falls Church, VA 22043.
Philip J. Hilts	"The New Battle over Handguns," *Good Housekeeping*, June 1997.
David Icke	"Take My Gun . . . Please," *Truth Seeker*, vol. 124, no. 2, 1997. Available from 16935 W. Bernardo Dr., #103, San Diego, CA 92127.
Holman W. Jenkins Jr.	"Guns vs. Hired Guns," *Wall Street Journal*, February 24, 1999.
John R. Lott Jr.	"How to Stop Mass Shootings," *American Enterprise*, July/August 1998.
John R. Lott Jr.	"Suits Targeting Gun Makers Are off the Mark," *Wall Street Journal*, March 3, 1999.
John R. Lott Jr. and David B. Mustard	"Crime, Deterrence, and Right-to-Carry Concealed Handguns," *Journal of Legal Studies*, January 1997.
Matthew Miller	"L.A. Law," *New Republic*, February 22, 1999.
New Republic	"An Uncivil Action," March 1, 1999.

Grover G. Norquist   "Have Gun, Will Travel," *American Spectator*, November 1998.

Daniel D. Polsby   "From the Hip," *National Review*, March 24, 1997.

David E. Rosenbaum   "The Gun Debate Has Two Sides. Now, a Third Way," *New York Times*, May 23, 1999.

Vincent Schiraldi   "Maryland Gun Laws: It Works!" *Washington Post*, June 7, 1998.

Bill F. Seaman Jr.   "The Philadelphia Experiment: Gun Control or Crime Control?" *Shield*, Fall 1998.

Gordon Witkin   "Handgun Stealing Made Easy," *U.S. News & World Report*, June 9, 1997.

Index